The Open University
Mathematics: a third-level course
M357   Data Models and Databases

GW00374188

BLOCK II
DATA MODELS

PART 1
CONCEPTUAL DATA MODELS

Prepared by David Benyon for the Course Team

The Open University

The course team

Mike Newton, chairman
David Benyon, author
Jan Bright, BBC
Ian Cooke, staff tutor
Sue Dobson, graphic artist
Judy Emms, staff tutor
Mike Field, academic editor
Janet Findlay, course coordinator
Adam Gawronski, ACS
John Jaworski, BBC
Roger Lowry, publishing editor
Diane Mole, designer
Hugh Robinson, author
Pip Surgey, BBC
Ray Weedon, author
Kambiz Yazdanjoo, ACS

External assessor

Peter Hitchcock, University of York

The main course components

Block I The database environment

Block II Data models

Part 1 Conceptual data models
Part 2 Logical database theories
Part 3 Facts, dependencies and data models

Block III Using database management systems

Part 1 Database design and use
Part 2 Using SQL
Part 3 SQL database management

Block IV Managing databases

The Open University, Walton Hall, Milton Keynes, MK7 6AA.

First published 1990. Reprinted 1993.

Copyright © 1990 The Open University.

Designed by the Graphic Design Group of the Open University.

Printed and bound in the United Kingdom by Staples Printers Rochester Limited, Neptune Close, Medway City Estate, Frindsbury, Rochester, Kent ME2 4LT.

ISBN 0 7492 2022 8

This item forms part of an Open University course. The main components of the course are listed above. If you would like to buy this or other Open University material, please write to Open University Educational Enterprises Ltd, 12 Cofferidge Close, Stony Stratford, Milton Keynes MK11 1BY, Great Britain. If you wish to enquire about enrolling as an Open University student, please write to The Admissions Office, The Open University, PO Box 48, Walton Hall, Milton Keynes, MK7 6AB, Great Britain.

CONTENTS

STUDY GUIDE

Block II is in three parts and is about data models. The whole block constitutes four units of work, as indicated in the study chart opposite.

This first part, Part II.1, is about conceptual data models and constitutes one unit of work. In particular it is about the entity–attribute–relationship data model (the EAR model).

Section 1 provides a brief introduction to the notion of models as abstractions and to data models in particular. In Section 2 we provide an overview of the EAR data model. Sections 3 and 4 consider the three basic constructs of the EAR model, entities, attributes and relationships, in detail. In Section 5 the discussions of the previous sections are brought together to provide you with practice in producing EAR models starting from given requirements. Sections 1 to 4 should require about one and a half hours of study each. Section 5 should require about two hours.

There are no computer activities or Everest readings associated with this part. The one television programme associated with this part, TV3, illustrates the use of an EAR model in a particular organization.

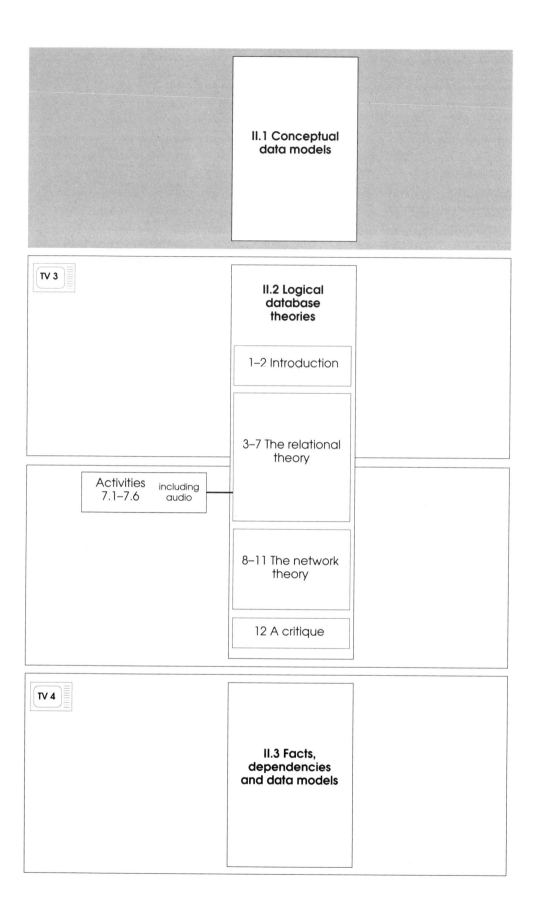

II.1 Conceptual data models

TV 3

II.2 Logical database theories

1–2 Introduction

3–7 The relational theory

Activities 7.1–7.6 including audio

8–11 The network theory

12 A critique

TV 4

II.3 Facts, dependencies and data models

INTRODUCTION TO BLOCK II

In Block I we considered the class of data processing systems which are the subject of this course — namely database systems. Such systems are characterized by a shared pool of data (the database) and by a multiplicity of users who have differing requirements of that database. Blocks II and III address the question of how to develop and construct a database so that it will meet the needs of the users. In Block II, we concentrate on obtaining an appropriate and accurate representation of the structure and semantics (i.e. meaning) of the data which the users require.

Block II consists of three parts. Part 1 concentrates on a technique for representing the structure and semantics of data in a form which is independent of any particular database management system (DBMS). Part 2 examines the capabilities of two general DBMS approaches to the representation of the structure and semantics of data in a formal manner. Part 3 takes a general look at of the relationship between data structure and semantics.

The stages in developing a database are shown in the figure below. We start at the point where an organization has identified some *applications* which are to be supported by developing a database. Further applications are anticipated as the database evolves. On the basis of these applications, the organization's *data requirements* are identified. The given data requirements now have to be represented structurally as a *database definition*, using a data definition language (DDL). This database definition describes the logical and physical structure of the actual *database*.

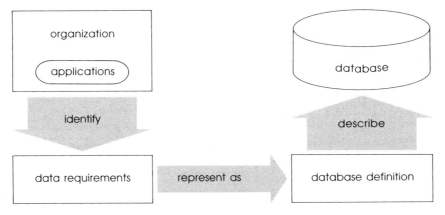

The stages in developing a database.

In this block we are concerned with the line labelled 'represent as' in the figure. We take as our starting point the data requirements of the organization and stop just short of database definition. The identification of data requirements is beyond the scope of this course, and so is not dwelt on here or elsewhere in the course. Database definition will be discussed in Block III, where you will study a DBMS language which includes a DDL.

1 INTRODUCTION

One of the stages shown in the figure in the Introduction to this block is the representation of data requirements as a database definition. In fact this stage involves a number of different representations, each of which has a role to play in the definition of a database. In this section we shall see how each of these representations is an *abstraction* from an organization's known needs and how these representations lead to a database definition. In particular we shall see how some of these abstractions are types of *data model*.

1.1 Towards a database definition

Figure 1.1 is an extended version of the figure in the Introduction to this block. It illustrates the six *processes* (numbered 1 to 6) which are involved in moving from the identification of the application requirements within an organization to a formal database definition. It also shows the five representations, or *abstractions* (labelled A to E), which may be produced and how these processes and representations are related. Figure 1.1 is still a simplification of the design process, as it ignores a number of aspects of database design (e.g. the development of userschemas and the needs of application programs), but it serves to highlight the steps which concern us in this block.

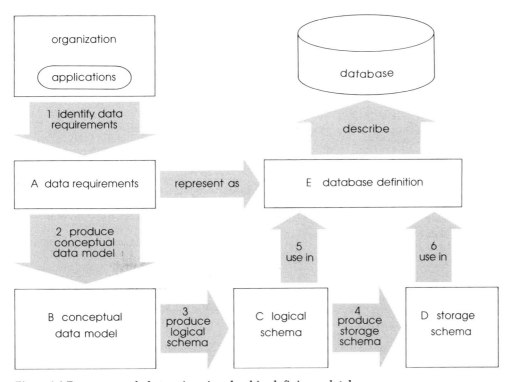

Figure 1.1 Processes and abstractions involved in defining a database.

First, the data requirements must be identified. This is part of the database system design process usually referred to as *systems analysis*. The outcome of systems analysis is a specification of all the processing, data and user requirements which the database system is to support. Our interest in systems analysis in this block concerns solely the **data requirements**, which we shall define as a statement of the data needed to satisfy the needs of the variety of users in an organization, together with a statement of the rules, or **constraints**, which apply to that data.

For example, from the university example which you were introduced to in Block I, the following data requirements can be deduced:

> Each course which is available for study has a course code, a course title and a credit value. Students may not enrol for more than three credits' worth of courses at any one time.

These data requirements demonstrate the need for the *data items* course code, course title and credit value and for the enforcement of the *constraint* that students may not enrol for more than three credits' worth of courses at any one time. This first process, the identification of data requirements, is beyond the scope of this course, and so statements of data requirements will provide the *starting point* for much of your work in this part.

Second, a conceptual data model is produced from the data requirements. The purpose of producing such a model is to focus on the essential *concepts* embodied in the data requirements. These essential concepts may be entities (such as 'course' and 'student' in the example above), attributes of entities (such as 'course code', 'course title' and 'credit value') or relationships between entities.[1] A **conceptual data model**, then, is a formal representation of the essential aspects of the data requirements.[2] A conceptual data model represents the structure and semantics of the data, but without concern for how these may be realized by any particular type of software system such as a DBMS. It is this second process, the production of the conceptual data model, that will be our main concern in this part.

Third, a logical schema is designed. This third process considers how the data structure and semantics specified in the conceptual data model can be represented given the capabilities of a particular type of DBMS. Different types of DBMS vary in their ability to represent data structures and semantics according to their underlying *logical database theory*. You will study logical database theories in Part 2 of this block.

Fourth, a storage schema is designed. This fourth process concentrates on the methods of storage offered by a particular DBMS. Storage and logical schemas can then be used (processes 5 and 6) in the production of the formal database definition, which describes the structure of the database using the data definition language (DDL) provided as part of a particular DBMS language. You will study some aspects of storage schemas and a DBMS language which includes a DDL in Block III.

Each of the representations (A to E in Figure 1.1) produced during the database design process is an **abstraction**, that is, a simplified representation of a system that emphasizes some of the details of the system while suppressing others. Data requirements are an abstraction, based on an organization's identified applications, which emphasizes the properties of the data structure of these applications, while suppressing the details of processing. A conceptual data model is an abstraction, based on the data requirements, which emphasizes the data semantics and natural data structure occurring in the data requirements, while suppressing details of how they may be realized in DBMSs. A logical schema is an abstraction, based on the conceptual data model, which emphasizes the representation of the data structure and semantics according to the logical capabilities of a particular type of DBMS, while suppressing storage details and the way the schema is to be used in database definition. A storage schema is an abstraction which emphasizes storage details. Database definition is the final abstraction, whereby the logical and storage schemas are represented in the DDL of the particular DBMS being used to implement the database.

---

[1] Entities, attributes and relationships were defined informally in Section 1.3.1 of Block I. These informal definitions are formalized in Sections 2–4 of this part.

[2] Note that here we are referring to a conceptual model of *data*, not, as in Everest Chapter 3 and in Block I Section 3, to a conceptual model of a *database management system*.

Each of these abstractions is generally concerned with *types* of data rather than with *occurrences* of data. For example, for the university database, these abstractions will reflect the fact that there is to be data on courses and students, but they do not need to reflect the fact that one of the courses is a Semantics course or that there is a student named Akeroyd.

1.2 Abstractions and models

The notion of an abstraction is an important one in this block, so it is worth spending a little time looking at abstraction in more detail. The previous subsection defined an abstraction as a simplified representation of a system that emphasizes some of the details of the system while suppressing others. A good abstraction is one in which information which is significant *for the purpose at hand* is emphasized and details which are immaterial or diversionary for that purpose are suppressed. In representing a system there are frequently a number of different, but related, purposes which have to be met. Hence a number of abstractions may be required for a given system, as is the case when we try to develop a database definition from the data requirements of an organization.

Models are a particularly useful and common form of abstraction. A **model** is a representation of something, constructed and used for a particular purpose. We use models constantly in all walks of life because they present a simplified view of the world, which highlights the parts which interest us. In particular, any design work involves the production of models: e.g. an architect's drawings, an artist's sketches, a mathematical model of an engineering project, a scale model of a new housing development, and so on. A good model is accurate enough to reflect the important features of the system being modelled, but simple enough to avoid confusion. A good model adopts a style of presentation which is suitable for its purpose. Examples of good models are provided by many of the diagrams in the four chapters of Everest you read in Block I.

A very familiar type of model is a map. Different maps help to illustrate the different levels and types of abstractions. Road maps ignore the details of the streets in a town, so that the traveller can concentrate on the major routes. However, street plans provide the detail which is required to find your way around a town. The map of the London Underground is a classic example of a model suited to its purpose. Everyone knows that the railway lines are not straight, and the stations are not regular distances apart. But the Underground map can represent them like this because attention is then focused on the important features of the Underground system: the order of the stations and the intersections of the lines.

Different models representing different levels of abstraction are required at different times. At one extreme there is the very abstract, high-level, model of the situation which is required to put relevant parts into perspective. At the other extreme is the more concrete, low-level, model required to provide the detail needed to complete the description. There may be several intermediate models required to provide a smooth transition between these two extremes. Consider, for example, the different representations of the UK provided by high-level models such as weather maps, contour maps and traffic density maps and low-level models such as Ordnance Survey 1:50000 maps, street plans and so on. In the middle lie the abstractions such as road and rail maps. To produce a database definition, Figure 1.1 shows the need for models at three levels, based on the data requirements. These are the conceptual data model, the logical schema and the storage schema.

The process of the construction of models is often just as important as the finished model. For example, in order to draw a road map you are forced to consider what are the important features of roads: where they intersect, how they relate to the major landmarks such as buildings, rivers, railways, and so on. You are forced to express your knowledge clearly and unambiguously, and in doing so you frequently expose gaps in your understanding. The *entity–relationship diagram*, which will be introduced in Section 2, is a highly effective exploratory model which helps the data modeller to understand the meaning and structure of data as expressed by the data requirements of a system. When completed, the entity–relationship diagram provides a 'map' of the system which can be followed to help ensure a complete and accurate representation of those data requirements.

Exercise 1.1

For the following description, identify the different models that are produced and the purpose(s) to which they are put:

> A car designer has been commissioned to design a new sports car. He sketches a few designs on paper and shows them to the other designers. They make various comments and, as a result, changes are made to the designs. Finally the designer is satisfied with three of the designs and produces scale drawings which are sent to the firm's model-maker. Wooden scale models of the designs are produced and are sent to marketing personnel for their reaction. The scale models are also subjected to wind tunnel experiments to investigate the aerodynamics of the design.

Exercise 1.2

Referring to the solution to Exercise 1.1:

(a) Why did the designer not produce scale drawings straight away?

(b) Why were the scale drawings not sent to marketing personnel?

(c) Why is a scale model suitable for testing in a wind tunnel?

The production and use of models is important in many disciplines in order to enhance understanding and to abstract important features, so that we are able to 'see the wood from the trees'. However, care must always be taken that the level and type of abstraction, and the style of the representation, is suitable for the purpose.

Returning to *our* purpose — representing data requirements as a database definition — you should be able to appreciate the analogy with the car designer of Exercises 1.1 and 1.2. A conceptual data model is a high-level model suitable for exploring alternative representations of the data requirements, yet is precise enough to be used as the basis for a logical schema. The logical schema is a representation of the conceptual data model tailored to suit a particular type of DBMS, but which ignores details of the 'interior', i.e. storage considerations. A conceptual data model uses a form of representation — a diagram and some text — which is suitable for providing an immediate, overall picture of the data requirements. The logical schema uses a form of representation — syntactically precise text — which is suitable for translating into the final database definition.

In common with some other forms of abstraction, the development of conceptual data models involves three general processes: *classification*, *generalization* and *aggregation*.[3]

---

[3] Much of the discussion of these processes should remind you of the discussion of entities, attributes and relationships in Block I.

Classification is the process of identifying individual objects as belonging to **classes** of objects. Alternatively, we may say that classification recognizes that different objects may be of the same **type**. For example, in the university, we would identify the people known as Akeroyd, Reeves and Thompson as all being students. The name of the class, or type, in this case, is Student. The particular people known as Akeroyd, Reeves and Thompson are **instances**, or **occurrences**, of the class.

Generalization is the process of identifying generic categories from classes of objects. Generalization recognizes characteristics which are common to a number of classes, or types, thus enabling a class of classes, known as a **generic class** or **generic type**, to be formed. For example, students, patients, doctors and nurses may be considered as **subclasses** or **subtypes** of the generic class or type 'person'. Person is thus a generalization of Student, Patient, Doctor and Nurse. Members of a generic class or type share some properties or characteristics. For example, all persons have the common properties of possessing a name and date of birth.

Aggregation is the process of collecting together information related to an object. For example, the object 'person' may be usefully viewed as an aggregation of the properties 'name', 'address', 'date of birth' and so on.

1.3 Data models

In your studies of other courses you may have come across *data flow models*. Such models concentrate on the the ways in which data is transformed by various processes, and as such are *processing models*. In this course, we are generally concerned with structure rather than processing — the structure of the data in the data requirements, the structures provided by logical database theories and the structure of the database — and so the models which interest us are *structural models* rather than processing models. In particular, in this block we shall concentrate on **data models**, which are models of the *structure* of data. By considering structure, data models not only enable us to model the structure of data but also enable us to capture the *semantics* of data.

Each of the representations B to E in Figure 1.1 is a data model. The conceptual data model represents the natural data structure in the data requirements. The logical schema represents that data structure as a logical data model in terms of the capabilities of a logical database theory. The storage schema represents that data structure as a physical data model in terms of the particular methods of storage available. The data definition, which is a representation of the logical schema and the storage schema (i.e. of the database schema) by means of the data definition language specific to a particular DBMS, represents that data structure as a data model specific to that DBMS.

Although we are concerned with developing data models, we must not lose sight of the fact that the database system is to be used by people and is to be implemented on a computer. The data models we develop must, therefore, serve the purposes of capturing the information which people require (and the different views required by different users) and of providing enough precision to be implemented by computer professionals.

The type of data model which we develop in this part — the conceptual data model — is an abstraction which is not constrained by the details of implementation; instead it focuses attention on the things of interest in the data requirements, the properties of those things and the relationships between those things. In addition, the conceptual data model is used by designers to help them understand the data, its meaning, interrelationships, characteristics and context. The conceptual data model must also provide a representation of the system suitable for translating into a logical schema. As you will see, the type of conceptual data model we discuss in this part — the *EAR model* — is particularly suited to these purposes.

The fact that conceptual data models look towards the 'real world' of data requirements, rather than towards the database definition, is important. While we expect conceptual data models to be implemented in some fashion, they need not be implemented using a DBMS, or indeed *any* software system. Conceptual data models represent *what* is needed, rather than *how* those needs may be met.

1.4 Summary of section

In this section we have provided an introduction to the process of designing a database. We have seen how a number of data models are required in order to move from a specification of data requirements to a concrete definition of a database. We have also looked at some general issues of modelling and processes of abstraction which are relevant to the production of data models in general and of conceptual data models in particular.

Having completed this section you should now be able to:

1 Understand what is meant by abstraction, and realize that this can involve the processes of classification, generalization and aggregation.

2 Explain what is meant by a model in general and a data model in particular.

3 Describe in general terms the various processes and data models involved in moving from the data requirements of an organization to the definition of a database.

2 ENTITY–ATTRIBUTE–RELATIONSHIP MODELS

In this course we shall examine in detail only one type of conceptual data model, known as the *entity–attribute–relationship (EAR) model*. In this section we provide an overview of the EAR model. In Section 2.1 we identify the principle components of the model. In Section 2.2 we focus attention on its diagrammatic component, the E–R diagram. Note that much of the teaching in this section is by example; a more formal and detailed approach to some of the ideas is given in Sections 3 and 4.

2.1 Principle components

The three fundamental concepts in the EAR model are *entities*, *attributes* and *relationships*. **Entities** are things which hold particular interest for the organization and about which data is to be recorded. **Attributes** are the properties, or characteristics, of entities. **Relationships** are associations between entities.[4]

To illustrate these concepts, recall the hospital example from Block I. We saw that the things of interest in that organization included patients, consultants, clinic appointments and wards. Patients have properties such as the patient number, name and address. Consultants have the properties name, title and specialism. The date and time are properties of clinic appointments, and the ward number, ward type and number of beds are properties of each ward. We also saw that patients *book* clinic appointments and *attend* for their appointments, that consultants *take* clinic appointments and that wards are *occupied by* patients. On the basis of this information, two of the entities that would form part of the EAR model of the hospital system are Patient and ClinicAppointment. Three of the attributes of the entity Patient would be PatientNumber, Name and Address; two of the attributes of the entity ClinicAppointment would be Date and Time. Two of the relationships would be Books (between Patient and ClinicAppointment) and Attends (also between Patient and ClinicAppointment). Notice that we have used the convention that each entity, attribute and relationship is written with an initial capital letter for each new word and with words concatenated.

SAQ 2.1 Based on the information in the preceding paragraph:

(a) Find two other entities for the EAR model of the hospital system.

(b) Propose suitable attributes for these two other entities.

(c) Find two other relationships for the EAR model of the hospital system, stating which pairs of entities are associated by them.

Solution

(a) Two other entities are Consultant and Ward.

(b) Attributes of the entity Consultant are Name, Title and Specialism and attributes of the entity Ward are WardNumber, WardType and NumberOfBeds.

(c) Two other relationships are Takes between the entities Consultant and ClinicAppointment and OccupiedBy between the entities Ward and Patient. ∎

---

[4] Compare these definitions with those given by Everest and reprinted on page 13 of Block I.

In terms of the discussion of abstraction in Section 1.2, each entity, attribute and relationship in an EAR model is a class or type of object. Thus, for example, the entity Patient in the EAR model of the hospital system is the class of all patients in the hospital; each individual patient is thus an **occurrence** or **instance** of that class. To emphasize this, some authors refer to **entity classes** or **entity types** rather than to entities; similarly they refer to to **attribute classes** or **attribute types** and to **relationship classes** or **relationship types**.[5] And indeed we shall sometimes use this terminology in this course when it is important to distinguish between the abstract concept of an entity, attribute or relationship and concrete occurrences or instances of such concepts, which we shall refer to as **entity occurrences** or **entity instances**, **attribute occurrences** or **attribute instances** or **attribute values** and **relationship occurrences** or **relationship instances**.[6] You too should be careful to distinguish between types and occurrences in your own work whenever there is a possibility of confusion.

In choosing the names for entities, attributes and relationships we try to find short but meaningful words or phrases. The names of entities and relationships need to be distinct within an EAR model, as do the names of the attributes of any particular entity. However, the name of an attribute of one entity may be the same as the name of an attribute of another entity within the same EAR model, since these attribute names can be distinguished by referring to the entity to which they belong. It is thus permissible to have Name as the name of an attribute of Patient and of Consultant in the EAR model of the hospital system.[7] We generally use entity names in the singular, e.g. Patient rather than Patients, because an entity type represents the *characteristics* of occurrences of that entity, and is not a *collection* of occurrences of that entity; i.e. the entity name is the name of the class of these occurrences. You may find it helpful to note that the names of entities and attributes are usually nouns, such as Patient, Consultant, PatientNumber, Address and Specialism, while the names of relationships are often verbs, such as Attends and OccupiedBy.

Although the the EAR model is *based on* entities, attributes and relationships, it is rather more than *just* entities, attributes and relationships. If it is to be a good model, as defined in Section 1.2, then it must emphasize those features of the system that are significant for the purpose at hand while suppressing those that are immaterial. The purpose of developing a conceptual data model is to represent the structure and semantics of the system as described in the data requirements. Saying simply, for example, that Patient and ClinicAppointment are entities and that a Patient Books a ClinicAppointment is not enough. We need a more formal and precise definition of the *meaning* of these things. We need to say exactly what the attributes of each entity are and under what circumstances occurrences of entities participate in the relationships. We also need to specify any constraints which are to be imposed on the data (for example, in the hospital there is a constraint that the number of patients occupying a ward cannot exceed the number of beds in that ward). Most importantly, we need to have a diagrammatic convention which allows the important features to stand out and provides a picture of the system so that we can see quickly how the entities are related to each other.

The **EAR model** thus consists of:

- A diagram showing the entities and relationships. (This is the E–R diagram and is introduced in Section 2.2.)

---

[5] Everest, for example, sometimes uses this terminology, as you may have noticed during your study of Block I.

[6] This discussion of the difference between types and occurrences parallels the discussion of record types and record occurrences in Section 1.3.1 of Block I.

[7] Though of course there is no reason why we should not use the names PatientName and ConsultantName if we prefer.

14

- A formal description of each entity in terms of its attributes. (This is covered in Section 3.)

- Descriptions of the meaning of relationships. (This is covered in Section 4.)

- Descriptions of any constraints on the system and of any assumptions made. (This is covered in Section 5.)

2.2 The E–R diagram

The **entity–relationship (E–R) diagram** shows the entities and relationships in the EAR conceptual data model. It does *not* show the attributes; hence the name E–R diagram rather than EAR diagram. It forms an essential part of the EAR model, but must not be equated with the complete EAR model because it cannot capture all the details of a system; nor does it provide a formal definition of the entities and relationships. The E–R diagram is particularly useful at the early stages of developing an EAR model as it provides an immediate, graphical representation of the main things of interest — entities and the relationships between those entities. When the EAR model is complete, the E–R diagram provides a useful map of the system.

The university

In Section 1.4 of Block I, we introduced the university system and described the activities which had to be supported by that system. In Activity 2 of that block you had experience of using the university database. In this subsection we look again at the university, but this time concentrate on the data requirements, with a view to producing an E–R diagram of the system.

The following description of the university's data requirements is typical of the data requirements of an organization, from which an EAR model can be developed:

The university system data requirements

A distance learning university needs to keep details of staff and students, the courses which are available and the performances of students on courses. Students are initially registered and issued with a student identification number. Students do not need to enrol for any courses on initial registration. The region which they are in is recorded along with the year of registration and the student's name. Each member of staff has a staff number and name recorded and also belongs to a region. Each staff member may act as a counsellor to one or more students and/or may tutor one or more students on courses. Each student has one counsellor, and may have a tutor for each course on which he/she is enrolled. Staff members may only tutor and counsel students who are located in the same region as the member of staff.

Each course which is available for study is given a course code, a title and a credit value. This value is 0.5 for a half-credit course and 1 for a full-credit. Each course may have no, one or many students enrolled on it. Students may not enrol for more than three credits' worth of courses at any one time. A full-credit course may have up to five TMAs (tutor marked assignments) and a half-credit course up to three TMAs. Each TMA is given a number between 1 and 5. The grade which a student obtains (expressed as a mark out of 100) for a given TMA on a given course is recorded.

SAQ 2.2 Identify four entities to be used in the University EAR model, giving each a suitable name.

Solution The four most obvious entities are Student, Course, Staff and TMAGrade. ∎

Do not be concerned if you identified other entities, or did not identify some of the ones which we chose. Identifying entities from data requirements is a skill which you will develop during this part. However, if your solution did not agree with ours, reread the data requirements now to satisfy yourself that Student, Course, Staff and TMAGrade are indeed types of things which we want to store data about. If you think that you have identified other entities, you may be right! For the time being we will just consider the four entities listed above.

To start drawing the E–R diagram, we represent each entity by drawing a *soft box* (a rectangle with rounded corners) around each entity name, as shown in Figure 2.1. The layout of the boxes at this stage is (almost) random. It is most important to remember that each soft box represents an entity type, not an entity occurrence; so, for example, the box named Student represents characteristics common to *all* the students, not any particular student.

Figure 2.1 The initial entities in the E–R diagram for the university.

Having seen how how entities are represented on the E–R diagram, let us now turn to the representation of relationships.

In the university example, there is a relationship between the entities Student and Staff indicated in the data requirements by the statements 'each staff member may act as a counsellor' and 'each student has one counsellor'. As with all relationships, this can be expressed in two ways, as a relationship between Student and Staff or as a relationship between Staff and Student. In other words, we can express the relationship by saying that a student is *counselled by* a staff member or by saying that a staff member *counsels* students. Now, because all relationships are *bidirectional*, we can choose either expression of the relationship as the source of the name of the relationship. Following Section 2.1, where it was suggested that the names of relationships should be short but meaningful words or phrases, we choose Counsels for the name of the relationship between Staff and Student, since this is shorter than the alternative IsCounselledBy. We emphasize at this point that, although the name of a relationship is likely to imply a relationship between two entities in one direction only, the reverse relationship must also hold; relationships are *always* bidirectional.[8]

When we come to represent relationships on the E–R diagram, we need to know more than the name of the relationship and the names of the entities which it relates. It is useful on the E–R diagram to be able to distinguish between

---

[8] Note that, provided there is only *one* relationship between two entities, such as Staff and Student, it is sometimes convenient and unambiguous to refer to that relationship as the Staff:Student relationship, for example.

relationships which can potentially involve only one entity occurrence from relationships which can potentially involve many entity occurrences. For example, a student has only one counsellor and so each Student occurrence will be related to only one Staff occurrence via the Counsels relationship; but each Staff occurrence can potentially be related to several Student occurrences, because each staff member may potentially counsel several students. We say that the *degree* of the Counsels relationship between Staff and Student is *one-to-many*.[9] Three **degrees** of relationship may be distinguished, as shown in Figure 2.2. The 'many' end of a relationship always ends in a *trident* or *crow's foot*.

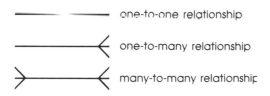

Figure 2.2 Notation for expressing the three degrees of relationship.

In the E–R diagram, each relationship is represented using the notation shown in Figure 2.2 together with the name of the relationship. Thus the Counsels relationship between the entities Staff and Student would be written and interpreted as illustrated in Figure 2.3.

Interpretation The degree of the Counsels relationship between Staff and Student is one-to-many. A member of staff may counsel many students. A student has at most one counsellor.

Figure 2.3 The Counsels relationship.

Notice the interpretation in Figure 2.3. We have said that a member of staff *may* counsel many students. This does *not* mean that *every* member of staff counsels many students. There may be members of staff who counsel only one student or none at all! Similarly the diagram is interpreted to mean that a student has *at most* one counsellor. It does not (yet) show that each student must have a counsellor. In other words, when discussing degree, the word 'one' means 'at most one' and the word 'many' means 'potentially many'.

Armed with the notions of entities and of relationships of degree one-to-one, one-to-many or many-to-many, we can now produce an initial E–R diagram for the university example, by adding the appropriate relationships between the entities of Figure 2.1. This is shown in Figure 2.4. Notice that this is an *initial* E–R diagram, and we are likely to want to change it before we are confident that it truly represents all the structure and semantics of the data requirements.

Figure 2.4 may be interpreted as follows. A student may study many courses and a course may have many students studying it. A student may be counselled by a member of staff and a member of staff may counsel many students.

---

[9] One-to-many relationships may also be referred to as many-to-one relationships, depending on the order in which the related entities are referred to. Thus the degree of the Counsels relationship between Student and Staff is many-to-one.

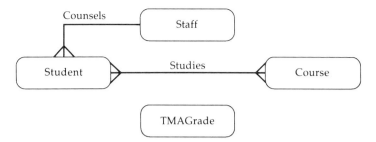

Figure 2.4 An initial E–R diagram for the university.

As it stands, Figure 2.4 is clearly an unsatisfactory representation of the data requirements of the university. We have not yet established a relationship between TMAGrade and any of the other entities and we do not have a relationship representing the fact that members of staff tutor students. In the data requirements we are told that 'each student ... may have a tutor for each course on which he/she is enrolled' and that 'the grade which a student obtains ... for a given TMA on a given course is recorded'. It appears, then, that both the 'tutors' relationship and the relationship which TMAGrade has with the Student and Course entities is not with either of them alone but with a combination of both. This suggests therefore that an object of interest in the university is an 'enrolment', representing a student taking a course, and that we should introduce an entity named Enrolment into our EAR model. The Enrolment entity will have a relationship with the Course entity, which we will call StudiedBy, and it will also have a relationship with the Student entity, which we will call Enrolled.

SAQ 2.4 Enrolment is an entity each occurrence of which represents *a* student taking *a* course. What is the degree of the Enrolled relationship which Enrolment has with the entity Student? What is the degree of the StudiedBy relationship which Enrolment has with the entity Course?

Solution The relationship between Enrolment and Student is many-to-one, since an Enrolment occurrence is related to a single Student occurrence, but a Student occurrence may have many Enrolment occurrences related to it (one for each course which the student is taking). The relationship between Enrolment and Course is many-to-one, since an Enrolment occurrence relates to only one Course occurrence, but a Course occurrence may have many Enrolment occurrences related to it (one for each student taking the course). ∎

SAQ 2.5 Draw an E–R diagram for the part of the university system which involves the entities Student, Course and Enrolment and the relationships Enrolled and StudiedBy.

Solution

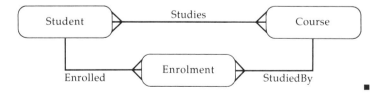

∎

An important point to note about the solution to SAQ 2.5 is that the Studies relationship is now *redundant*, because what it represents is precisely equivalent to that which is represented by the Enrolment entity. Both Studies and Enrolment represent the same part of the data requirements: the courses which a student is taking and the students who are taking a course. Redundancy in a conceptual data model is to be avoided, as it leads to unnecessary complexity, and can lead to a loss of integrity; so we should remove the Studies relationship from the model.[10]

Now, the inclusion of the Enrolment entity enables us to add to the diagram the two relationships which are missing — the relationship between TMAGrade and Enrolment, which we will call Awarded, and the relationship to represent 'tutors', which we will call Tutors.

SAQ 2.6 What is the degree of the relationship Awarded between Enrolment and TMAGrade?

Solution Each TMAGrade occurrence is related to only one Enrolment occurrence (i.e. is related to only one student taking one course), but every Enrolment occurrence is potentially related to several TMAGrade occurrences. Therefore the degree of the Awarded relationship between Enrolment and TMAGrade is one-to-many. ∎

SAQ 2.7 The data requirements tell us that 'each staff member ... may tutor one or more students on courses' and that 'each student ... may have a tutor for each course on which he/she is enrolled'. Develop an E–R diagram for this part of the data requirements.

Solution The important features here are that each student has at most one tutor for each course and that staff members may tutor many students. In the Tutors relationship, each Staff occurrence may be related to many Enrolment occurrences but each Enrolment occurrence is related to at most one Staff occurrence. Therefore the Tutors relationship between Staff and Enrolment is one-to-many. The E–R diagram is therefore as shown below:

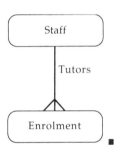

We are now in a position to put together a more complete E–R diagram for the university, as shown in Figure 2.5. This is not *the* complete E–R diagram for the university, as you will see later, but it is as far as we need go for the present.

You will notice from Figure 2.5 that each entity may be related to several other entities: for example, Enrolment is related to four entities. Indeed, pairs of entities may be related by more than one relationship. For example, suppose there were a relationship between Staff and Student other than Counsels; we would then add this relationship as a separate named line on the E–R diagram. Figure 2.5 also

---

[10] You will see later, in Section 4, that *any* many-to-many relationship, such as Studies, can — though need not — be replaced by an entity and two one-to-many relationships, such as Enrolment, Enrolled and StudiedBy.

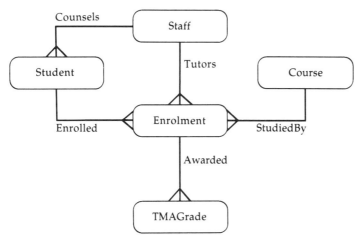

Figure 2.5 A more complete E–R diagram for the university.

demonstrates that, even with relatively simple E–R diagrams, it is important to try to ensure clarity by drawing the diagram so that related entities are adjacent to one another and so that relationship lines do not cross each other. It is also standard practice, as in Figure 2.5, to draw E–R diagrams so that the 'to-many' end of a one-to-many relationship line is lower than the 'to-one' end, whenever this can be achieved simply.

The hospital

Now, to give you practice in developing E–R diagrams, we return to the hospital example of Block I, part of which we summarize with the following, simplified data requirements:

The hospital system data requirements

Patients make clinic appointments to see a consultant. Each clinic appointment is taken by a single consultant. Each consultant sees one patient in each appointment. As a result of a clinic appointment, a patient may be admitted to a hospital ward. During their stay in hospital, each patient is under the care of a single consultant, but a consultant may be responsible for a number of patients. Each ward is staffed by a number of nurses, each of whom is assigned to a single ward.

Exercise 2.1

Use the above data requirements for the hospital system to do the following:

(a) Identify five entities and give them suitable names.

(b) Identify five relationships between the five entities you identified in (a). Give the relationships suitable names and find the degree of each. (In giving the degree, take care to show which is your first entity and which is your second.)

(c) Draw an E–R diagram for the hospital system, using the entities and relationships you identified in (a) and (b).

Occurrence diagrams

The E–R diagrams that we have been developing are, strictly speaking, entity–relationship *type* diagrams. Such diagrams show only the generality of entities and not specific occurrences that might actually be required to be recorded as data at any particular time. This statement should not be interpreted as a criticism of the E–R diagram, because to record such details would obscure its purpose. However, to consolidate your understanding of the differences between entity and relationship types and their occurrences, let us look at some particular data from the university example, shown in Figure 2.6.

Jennings	Counsels	Akeroyd
Heathcote	Counsels	Thompson
Heathcote	Counsels	Ellis
Jennings	Counsels	Gillies
Heathcote	Counsels	Reeves
Heathcote	Counsels	Urbach

Figure 2.6 Some data from the university example.

Each line of Figure 2.6 describes an occurrence of the Counsels relationship, giving six occurrences of the Counsels relationship in all. Two occurrences of the Staff entity are represented — Heathcote and Jennings — and six occurrences of the Student entity — Akeroyd, Thompson, Ellis, Gillies, Reeves and Urbach.

We can represent the relationship occurrences in Figure 2.6 on an **E–R occurrence diagram** by linking the entity occurrences with lines, one line for each occurrence of the relationship. The names of the entity and relationship types are also included in the diagram, as shown in Figure 2.7.

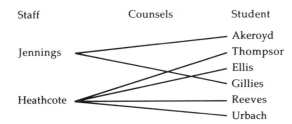

| Staff | Counsels | Student |

Jennings		Akeroyd
		Thompson
		Ellis
		Gillies
Heathcote		Reeves
		Urbach

Figure 2.7 The E-R occurrence diagram for the data in Figure 2.6.

Thus the difference between the representation of a relationship in an E–R occurrence diagram (such as Figure 2.7) and its representation in an E–R diagram (such as Figure 2.3) is that the E–R diagram illustrates the general case, the entity and relationship *types*, whereas the E–R occurrence diagram shows some specific *occurrences* of those types.

Exercise 2.2

Consider the following data for the university example:

Akeroyd studies Semantics. Ellis studies Syntax and Pragmatics. Reeves studies Semantics, Syntax and Pragmatics.

(a) Identify the entity occurrences in the data.

(b) What are the two entity types for which there are occurrences in this data? How many occurrences are there of each entity type?

(c) What is the relationship type for which there are occurrences in this data? How many occurrences are there of this relationship type?

(d) Draw an E–R occurrence diagram, in the style of Figure 2.7, for the entity and relationship occurrences identified in your solutions to (b) and (c).

(e) What can you deduce about the degree of the relationship you have identified?

There is an important lesson to be learnt from the solution to Exercise 2.2(e). Occurrences only show a 'snapshot' of the database, and the set of occurrences which we have available may not be a complete illustration of all the relationships which *may* exist. If we have more than one occurrence of a relationship between an occurrence of one entity and occurrences of another entity, then we *can* say that the relationship is 'to-many', as was the case in Exercise 2.2. However, if we have at most a single occurrence of a relationship between each occurrence of one entity and each occurrence of another entity, then we *cannot* say with certainty that the relationship is 'to-one', as other relationship occurrences may be introduced later which would contradict this 'to-oneness'.

Entity and relationship types are said to be (relatively) **time-invariant**. Occurrences, on the other hand, are **time-variable**. The set of occurrences of an entity will be different at different times, as courses change, students enrol and tutors come and go, for example. It can be very useful to examine occurrences of the entities and relationships which exist or which may exist, but when we model the data requirements we must base that model on the time-invariant entity and relationship types.

2.3 Summary of section

This section has provided an introduction to the entity–attribute–relationship (EAR) conceptual data model, which consists of the E–R diagram, a formal description of each entity in terms of its attributes, and textual descriptions of the meanings of relationships, of the system constraints and of any assumptions made.

The E–R diagram is a data model — a model of the structure of data. It focuses attention on the entities and relationships which are of interest in the data requirements. Relationships have a degree of one-to-one, one-to-many or many-to-many, highlighting whether each entity occurrence is associated with at most one or potentially more than one occurrence of another entity. Entities and relationships are given distinct, meaningful names.

The E–R diagram is a good model because it emphasizes the things which interest us for the purpose at hand, while suppressing the diversionary details. The purpose of the E–R diagram is to provide an immediate representation of the entities and relationships and to help examine alternative representations of the data requirements.

Having completed this section you should now be able to:

1 Identify likely entities from the data requirements for a small example situation.

2 Specify likely relationships between entities, and the degree of those relationships, for a small example situation.

3 Draw an E–R diagram from the data requirements for a small example situation.

3 ENTITIES AND THEIR ATTRIBUTES

In this section we develop the idea of entities and their attributes in more detail. We start in Section 3.1 by looking at the concept of an attribute, and then proceed in Section 3.2 to consider how attributes may be used to identify entities. Section 3.3 introduces notation for the formal definition of entities. The final subsection introduces the concept of an entity subtype.

3.1 Attributes

In Section 2.1, we defined an attribute as a property, or characteristic, of an entity. Attributes represent the data which is to be kept about entities.

SAQ 3.1 For each of the entities in the solution to SAQ 2.2, list the attributes which can be identified from the data requirements for the university system, given immediately before that SAQ, giving each attribute a suitable name.

Solution For the entity Student we have the following attributes:

StudentId — the student identification number;
Region — the region which the student is in;
Registered — the year of registration;
Name — the name of the student.

For the entity Staff we have:

StaffNo — the staff number;
Name — the name of the member of staff;
Region — the region which the member of staff belongs to.

For the entity Course we have:

CourseCode — the course code;
Title — the course title;
Credit — the credit value.

For the entity TMAGrade we have:

TMANo — the identifying number of the TMA;
Grade — the grade obtained by the student on the TMA. ∎

As with SAQ 2.2, your solution may not exactly match ours; nevertheless your attributes should be properties of the given entities. You should convince yourself that our chosen attributes are such properties.

As with entities and relationships, we have to be careful to distinguish between attribute *types*, the general categories of data, such as CourseCode, Title, etc., and the occurrences of those attributes, such as Semantics, Syntax and Pragmatics, which are occurrences of the attribute type Title. Occurrences of attributes are usually referred to as **attribute values**. Attribute types are classifications of the allowable attribute values. The set of allowable values for an attribute is known as the attribute's **value set**. Hence, the value set for Title could be {Semantics, Syntax, Pragmatics}; but it could of course include other titles that we happen not to have come across yet.

SAQ 3.2 What is the value set for the Credit attribute identified in SAQ 3.1?

Solution The value set for Credit is {0.5, 1}. ∎

Some value sets are very large and cannot be defined explicitly in terms of their members, as Title and Credit were above. In such cases the value set is defined as a *value range* or *value type*. For example, the value set for Name could be defined as any character string. We will not dwell on the concept of a value set at this point, as you will discover more about them in Part II.2 when you consider domains.

Attributes cannot exist independently of the entity of which they are a property. They have an important role to play in the definition of entities, as you will see below, but our main interest lies with the higher-level concept of an entity. In terms of the discussion of abstraction in Section 1.2, an entity is an *aggregation* of its attributes.

3.2 Identifiers

When we refer to an entity occurrence, we need to be sure that we know which occurrence we are talking about. In some of the examples above, we have not made this explicit. For example, if there were two or more students with the name Reeves, then the statement that Reeves studies Pragmatics and Reeves studies Syntax is ambiguous. Is it the same Reeves who studies two courses, or are there two students named Reeves each of whom studies one course? Furthermore there could even be two distinct courses both called Pragmatics. It is, therefore, vitally important that we can distinguish between entity occurrences. We do this by specifying one or more attributes for each entity, the values of which will enable us to identify, *uniquely*, each occurrence of the entity. The attribute(s) which fulfil this role are known as the entity **identifier**.

The identifier is a property of an entity. Sometimes an identifier is clear from the data requirements, such as in the university example where CourseCode identifies Course and StudentId identifies Student. Each value of CourseCode, for example, is always associated with the same single occurrence of the Course entity. However, the attribute Credit of the Course entity could not be an identifier because the values of Credit do not uniquely distinguish between occurrences of the Course entity. There are potentially several courses with the same credit rating.

Where a single-attribute identifier does not exist in the data requirements, we must look for a combination of attributes, known as a **composite identifier**, to fulfil the role. For example, a person's name is not usually considered to be a good identifier because there may come a time when data about another person with the same name is to be recorded. Address is not usually considered a good identifier because data about two people who live at the same address may need to be recorded. Name and Address taken together may be enough to identify an individual, or perhaps the composite identifier Name, Address and DateOfBirth may be required. A composite identifier is sometimes enclosed in brackets, e.g. (Name, Address, DateOfBirth). When choosing composite identifiers, it should be borne in mind that an identifier must be the *minimum* number of attributes required to distinguish unambiguously between entity occurrences.

Since we expect our system to evolve in time, care must be taken that any likely extensions to the system can be accommodated by the identifiers chosen. Thus, for example, if our current system requires only the details of rooms in a single building in an organization, then the number on the door may be sufficient as an identifier. However, if the system may sometime be expanded to encompass all the buildings in an organization, then the building number and the room number may both be needed.

Sometimes there is a choice of identifier for an entity. For example, a member of staff might be uniquely identified by a staff number or by the composite of name and department.[11] Where there is a genuine choice of identifiers, each is known as a **candidate identifier**. It is usual, in such circumstances, to choose the simplest attribute — staff number in this case — as the (actual) identifier.

If an attribute, or combination of attributes, is to be an identifier, then it is vital that each entity occurrence has a different value for that attribute. It follows that a value for (each part of) the identifier must *exist* for each entity occurrence. Absence of a value cannot identify anything! By a similar argument, identifiers should not be subject to change. For example, the use of a surname as an identifier is compromised if a person changes name on getting married. Thus an identifier should be *stable*.

SAQ 3.3 What are the four criteria for identifiers?

Solution

- Uniqueness. The value of the identifier must be unique to each entity occurrence.
- Minimality. The identifier should consist of the minimum number of attributes required in order to satisfy the uniqueness criterion, while bearing in mind the likely evolvability required.
- Existence. A value for (each part of) the identifier must exist for each entity occurrence.
- Stability. The values of identifiers should not be subject to change. ∎

Let us summarize the main points concerning identifiers. Every entity must have an identifier. The value of the identifier must be guaranteed to exist, to be stable and to be unique for each entity occurrence which *may* exist. There may be a single-attribute identifier for an entity which is clear from the data requirements, but if not then a minimum combination of attributes can be designated as the (composite) identifier. There may be a choice of identifier from among two or more candidate identifiers. It is important to consider the evolvability of the system when choosing identifiers. The concept of an identifier means that we can refer to entity occurrences simply by the value(s) of the identifying attribute(s).

Exercise 3.1 ———————————————————————————

In the hospital example, a clinic has a name such as Ear, Nose and Throat or Antenatal. These clinics are run several times a week but never more than once on the same day. The date and day name are recorded for each clinic. Each clinic is taken by one of the three consultants, Mr Watson, Dr Owen or Dr Cunningham. Each consultant has a specialism, name and title recorded.

(a) What are the entities in this description? What are the attributes of the entities?

(b) How would you identify the entity occurrences? What impact does the choice of identifier have on the evolvability of the system?

(c) What are the attribute values mentioned in this description? Do these values identify any entity occurrences?

---

[11] Note that, although name and department would be a composite identifier made up of two attributes, one more than the single-attribute identifier staff number, it is minimal in that neither name nor department can be omitted and still provide an identifier.

Exercise 3.2 ───

Since Enrolment is an entity for the university system, it must have an identifier. Use the attributes of the other entities for the university system, listed in the solution to SAQ 3.1, to help you to suggest what a suitable identifier might be. What assumption(s) does your choice of identifier make about the evolvability of the university system?

Exercise 3.3 ───

Suppose that the data requirements for the university system are extended to include the statement that 'each enrolment of a student on a course is given a unique enrolment number'.[12] Compare the use of the single attribute EnrolmentNumber with the use of the composite (StudentId, CourseCode) as possible identifiers for the Enrolment entity in each of the following two cases:

(a) the system keeps data on current enrolments only;

(b) data on previous enrolments is also to be kept.

Exercise 3.4 ───

The data requirements for the university system (see Section 2.2) state that each TMA is given a number between 1 and 5 (the attribute TMANo) and that the grade which a student obtains for a given TMA on a given course is recorded (the attribute Grade). We also know that the TMAGrade entity has a many-to-one relationship with Enrolment. What is the identifier of TMAGrade? Justify your answer.

A point to notice from Exercise 3.4 is that it may be necessary to introduce extra attributes into the list of attributes for an entity simply in order to identify it. In the case of the TMA entity, the answer to SAQ 3.1 may have led us to think that the only attributes of TMA were TMANo and Grade. However, we find that in order to identify the TMA entity we must introduce the perhaps less obvious attributes StudentId and CourseCode.

3.3 Entity definitions

Let us review what we know about entities and their attributes. First, an entity is something which is of interest in the data requirements and about which data is to be kept. As such it could be an object (e.g. car, machine, product, room), a person (e.g. customer, supplier, employee), an event (e.g. manufacturing operation, placement of order, holiday booking) or a more abstract concept (e.g. schedule, plan, department, order). Second, it must be possible to distinguish between entity occurrences. Third, an entity has at least one attribute — because it must have at least one attribute in order to identify occurrences — and will usually have other attributes as well.

   Attributes are the properties of entities, the things which we want to know about the entities. The possible values of attributes are defined by the value set associated with the attribute. Attribute values are the data which is to be recorded about the entity occurrences. The values of one or more attributes of each entity are used to identify entity occurrences.

───

[12] Note that this addition to the university system data requirements applies to this exercise only. Elsewhere we shall assume that enrolment numbers are not used.

You must keep a clear distinction between the entity and the identifier of the entity. An attribute (possibly a combination of attributes) will be used to identify and distinguish between entity occurrences, but the entity is not the attribute. For example, students are identified by a StudentId. Student is the entity; StudentId is an attribute of Student, *not* an entity. Similarly, a course is identified by a CourseCode. Course is the entity; CourseCode is an attribute of Course. An entity is certainly composed of attributes — representing the data which we want to keep about the entity — but the entity cannot be equated with the attributes. An entity is a different level of abstraction from an attribute, being an aggregation of its attributes.

We are now in a position to consider a formal representation of entities. Every entity has a name which is unique to the system and an identifying attribute (possibly composite) . In addition most entities will have a number of non-identifying attributes. The convention which we use for defining entities is shown below. The name of the entity is followed by the list of attributes, enclosed in parentheses, with the identifying attribute(s) placed first and underlined. Where all the attributes are not yet known, this is indicated by a row of dots.

EntityName (<u>IdentifyingAttribute1</u>, <u>IdentifyingAttribute2</u>, ...,
NonidentifyingAttribute1, NonidentifyingAttribute2, ...)

For example, we would define the Student and Course entities in the university system as follows:

Student (<u>StudentId</u>, Name, Registered, Region)
Course (<u>CourseCode</u>, Title, Credit)

Exercise 3.5

Produce entity definitions for the entities Staff, Enrolment and TMAGrade in the university system. (You may find it helpful to refer to the university system data requirements in Section 2.2 and the solutions to SAQ 3.1 and Exercises 3.2 and 3.4.)

3.4 Inside the hospital

The overall hospital system should be quite familiar to you by now. We shall now look in more detail at the hospital inpatient system, which is defined by the following data requirements:

The hospital inpatient system data requirements

The hospital is organized into a number of wards, each of which may be empty or may contain one or more patients. Each ward has a ward number and a name recorded, along with the number of beds in that ward. The number of patients occupying a ward cannot exceed the number of beds in the ward. Each ward is staffed by one or more nurses, one of whom is designated to supervise any others on that ward. Nurses have their staff number and name recorded and are assigned to a single ward.

Each patient in the hospital has a patient identification number, and their name, address and date of birth are recorded. Each patient is under the care of a single consultant and is assigned to a single ward. Each consultant is responsible for a number of patients and has a specialism recorded. Details of the junior doctors in the hospital, who are designated either as a registrar or as a houseman, are also recorded. Each doctor in the hospital (whether consultant or junior doctor) has a staff number and name recorded and belongs to a group, known as a team. Each team has a team code, consists of one or more housemen and registrars and is headed by a single consultant. Each consultant heads a team. The number of doctors in each team is recorded.

Each doctor may treat several patients and each patient may be treated by a number of doctors, all of whom must be members of the same team as the consultant who is responsible for the patient. The treatment which a patient receives includes the prescription of a certain dosage of drugs such as paracetamol, morphine, codeine, etc. Each drug has a code. Records are kept of the date and dosage of each drug treatment and of who prescribed it. Only doctors are allowed to prescribe treatment.

Exercise 3.6

Compile a list of likely entities for the hospital inpatient system, including a one-line meaning of each entity.

We cannot be sure yet that the list produced in answer to the previous exercise is the 'correct' list of entities. More importantly, perhaps, we cannot yet be sure that this is a *complete* list of entities. But it provides an adequate starting point for the development of an EAR conceptual data model.

Exercise 3.7

For each of the entities in our solution to Exercise 3.6, suggest a possible identifier for the entity, based on the data requirements for the hospital inpatient system.

3.5 Entity subtypes and supertypes

In the solution to Exercise 3.6, you may have been surprised to see Doctor, JuniorDoctor and Consultant listed as separate entities. Are not Consultant and JuniorDoctor simply special cases of Doctor and therefore the same entity? The answer to this question is that we do not yet know if they are better considered as separate entities or if they can be considered to be the same entity. This will become clearer as we develop the conceptual data model. The definitive answer will be provided when we discover if there is anything fundamentally different between the various types of doctor or whether they are essentially the same.

In fact, the answer may turn out to be a hybrid of these two extremes, in that certain attributes of doctors may be common to consultants and junior doctors and other attributes may be particular to only one of them. Similarly, it may be that all doctors will participate in some relationships whereas other relationships will only be applicable to particular types of doctor. This suggests that it can be useful to recognize the existence of entities which *share* certain properties, such as attributes or relationships, but which differ in others.

Thus, in the hospital inpatient system, we have already noted that it may be useful to identify Consultant and JuniorDoctor **subentities**, or **entity subtypes**, of the Doctor entity. The **superentity**, or **entity supertype**, Doctor is a *generalization* of the subentities, or entity subtypes, Consultant and JuniorDoctor. Note that subtypes must not overlap (i.e. they must be *disjoint*) and that between them they must cover all possible occurrences of the supertype. Thus, in the hospital system, all doctors must be either a consultant or a junior doctor, but not both, if Consultant and JuniorDoctor are to form the complete set of entity subtypes of the entity supertype Doctor.

SAQ 3.4 In the university system, it might seem possible to represent counsellors and tutors as subtypes of the entity Staff. Given our definition of a subtype, explain why this is not valid.

Solution It is not valid to use Counsellor and Tutor as subtypes of staff because a tutor may also be a counsellor. These subtypes would therefore not be disjoint subtypes of staff. ∎

The existence of entity subtypes can be useful in more accurately representing semantics in the EAR model. If a number of attributes or relationships are common to two or more entities, they are more economically represented by a single entity — the supertype. However, any differences must still be accommodated, and these differences are represented in the subtypes.

Consider the example of the entity Vehicle, being a generalization of the entity subtypes Car, Lorry and Bus, where these three subtypes account for all the kinds of vehicle of interest to an organization. Many properties are common to these three subtypes of Vehicle, but some properties are not. In the E–R diagram, we would model all these entities as shown in Figure 3.1. The subtypes are shown as smaller boxes inside a larger supertype box.

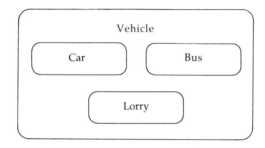

Figure 3.1 Representing subtypes and supertypes in an E–R diagram.

Let us now examine some possible relationships for the types of vehicle in Figure 3.1. Let us assume that we wish to model the fact that all these types of vehicle may be driven by persons but that only lorries may carry materials. There is a Drives relationship between Vehicle and the entity Person. There is also a Carries relationship between Lorry and the entity Materials. These relationships would appear as shown in Figure 3.2.

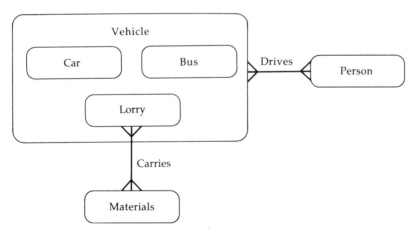

Figure 3.2 An E-R diagram showing subtypes and relationships.

Notice the economy of this E–R diagram, as a result of using the subtype concept. If the Vehicle supertype were not present there would have to be three separate Drives relationships, one each between Person and each of the subtypes.

All the attributes of the supertype, Vehicle in this case, must also be attributes of each of the subtypes; but each subtype may have additional attributes that it does not share with the other subtypes. Thus all vehicles will have attributes such as RegistrationNumber, EngineSize and Colour but only buses will have a SeatingCapacity attribute, for example. When writing formal entity definitions, there is no need to list any of the shared attributes of the subtypes other than those comprising the identifier; only those non-identifying attributes of subtypes that are not shared with other subtypes need be listed. The non-identifying shared attributes will appear in the definition of the entity supertype. Thus the entity definitions for the various kinds of vehicle would be something like this:

    Vehicle (<u>RegistrationNumber</u>, EngineSize, Colour, ...)
    Bus (<u>RegistrationNumber</u>, SeatingCapacity, ...)
    Lorry (<u>RegistrationNumber</u>, LoadingCapacity, ...)
    Car (<u>RegistrationNumber</u>, NumberOfDoors, ...)

Exercise 3.8

(a) Referring to the data requirements for the hospital inpatient system in Section 3.4, determine the degree of the following three relationships:

    (i) the relationship Treats between Doctor and Patient;

    (ii) the relationship HeadedBy between Team and Consultant;

    (iii) the relationship ConsistsOf between Team and JuniorDoctor.

(b) Draw an E–R diagram for the part of the hospital inpatient system which includes the entities Patient, Team and Doctor, the entity subtypes Consultant and JuniorDoctor and the relationships Treats, Heads and ConsistsOf. Give definitions for all five entities.

3.6 Summary of section

An entity has attributes which are the properties of that entity. The attribute values are drawn from a value set for the given attribute.

One vital attribute or combination of attributes of every entity is its identifier, the values of which must be capable of distinguishing between all possible occurrences of the entity. There may be more than one candidate identifier. An identifier must be unique and must exist for all possible occurrences, and should be minimal and stable.

A formal way of writing entity definitions consists of the entity name followed by the list of attributes in parentheses, usually beginning with the identifying attributes. The identifier, which may be composite, is underlined.

Entity subtypes are entity types that have all the attributes and relationships of the entity supertype but which also possess attributes and/or relationships of their own. Entity subtypes must be disjoint.

In our consideration of the concept of an entity, we have encountered all three of the processes of abstraction identified in Section 1.2. An entity type is a classification of the entity occurrences; an attribute type is a classification of the attribute values. Entity types are aggregations of attribute types. Entity supertypes are generalizations of entity subtypes.

Having completed this section you should now be able to:

1 Identify entities, attributes and entity identifiers from given data requirements.

2 Justify your choice of entities, attributes and entity identifiers for given data requirements.

3 Write formal entity definitions.

4 Describe and illustrate the concept of an entity subtype.

4 RELATIONSHIPS

In this section we shall first review and consolidate what you have already learnt about relationships. We shall then discuss the participation of entities in relationships and show how various conditions for participation can be represented on the E–R diagram. We shall next show how complex relationships can be decomposed into simple relationships. The section concludes with brief discussions of recursive relationships, that is relationships between an entity and itself, and of alternatives to the EAR conceptual data model.

4.1 Characteristics of relationships

A relationship is an association or link between two entities. There may be more than one relationship between the same pair of entities. Each relationship is given a distinct, meaningful name and is represented on an E–R diagram by a named line. A crow's foot or trident at the end of a relationship line indicates that the relationship is 'to-many'; otherwise the relationship is 'to-one'. All relationships are bidirectional, e.g. a student 'is counselled by' a member of staff and a member of staff 'counsels' students.

As with the other main components of the EAR conceptual data model — entities and attributes — we must be careful to distinguish between relationship *types* and relationship *occurrences*. In the university database, the fact that student s01, named Akeroyd, is counselled by staff member 3158, named Jennings, is an occurrence of the Counsels relationship. The relationship type — called Counsels in this case — expresses the fact that there *may* be associations between occurrences of Student and occurrences of Staff. A (time-invariant) relationship type represents a number (possibly zero) of (time-variable) relationship occurrences. As with entities, we can only learn a limited amount from looking at the occurrences of relationships; we need to consider the relationship types, the general rules, when developing the EAR model. The degree of a relationship describes the number of entity occurrences on one side of the relationship that may be associated with each entity occurrence on the other side of the relationship, and vice versa. Degree is expressed as one-to-one, one-to-many or many-to-many.

A one-to-one relationship between entities A and B is a relationship in which each occurrence of entity A may be associated with *at most one* occurrence of entity B *and* each occurrence of entity B may be associated with *at most one* occurrence of entity A. We often use the shorthand 1:1 for a one-to-one relationship.

When the 'at most one' rule does not apply to *one* side of the relationship, the relationship is said to be one-to-many (shorthand 1:n). This means that occurrences of entity A may be associated with *more than one* occurrence of entity B (but each occurrence of entity B may still be associated with *at most one* occurrence of entity A). Notice that occurrences of entity A do not have to be associated with any occurrences of entity B.

If the occurrences of the entities on both sides of the relationship may be associated with more than one of the entity occurrences on the other side, there is a many-to-many (shorthand m:n) relationship between the entities. m:n relationships are sometimes called **complex relationships** and 1:n relationships are sometimes referred to as **simple relationships**.

Exercise 4.1

Computers are sometimes allocated to individual persons in an organization. Nobody is allocated more than one computer. Some of the computers are mainframes and are not allocated to anybody. Some of the computers can have external disk drives attached to them and there are a few computers that can be attached to two drives at once. Any particular disk drive is attached to only one computer at any one time. There are several pieces of software available, not all of which will run on all the computers.

(a) Draw an E–R diagram based on the above data requirements, using the entities Person, Computer, DiskDrive and Software and the relationships Allocated between Person and Computer, IsAttachedTo between Computer and DiskDrive and Runs between Computer and Software.

(b) Describe the degree of each relationship and justify your choice by referencing the data requirements.

Notice that there are some facts that you were given in Exercise 4.1 that you were unable to reflect in your E–R diagram. For example, you were unable to reflect that mainframes are never allocated to anybody. In producing the E–R diagram you have to ensure that your diagram is consistent with the facts even if it cannot show them all.

SAQ 4.1 Continuing with the case described in Exercise 4.1, we now assume that at some point in time there are three Person occurrences, P1, P2 and P3, three Computer occurrences, C1, C2 and C3, three DiskDrive occurrences, D1, D2 and D3, and three Software occurrences, S1, S2 and S3. The relationship occurrences are as shown in the diagram below:

(a) How many occurrences are there of the IsAttachedTo relationship?

(b) Describe in English all the occurrences of the Runs relationship.

(c) What can be said about the Computer occurrence C3?

Solution

(a) Three. C1 is attached to D1, C2 to D2 and C2 to D3.

(b) Computer C1 runs the piece of software S1. Computer C2 runs the pieces of software S1, S2 and S3.

(c) Computer C3 is not allocated to any person, has no disk drive attached and runs none of the software. ∎

4.2 Participation in relationships

So far, relationships have been expressed in terms that show that entity occurrences need not participate in any of the relationships applicable to its entity type. We have said such things as, 'every occurrence of entity A *may* be associated with *more than one* occurrence of entity B'. It would be more helpful (since it represents more of the semantics) if we could represent further characteristics of the relationships and say such things as 'every occurrence of entity A is *always* associated with *precisely one* occurrence of entity B' or 'every occurrence of entity A *must* be associated with one occurrence of entity B, and *may* be associated with many'. In order to capture these additional semantics in the EAR conceptual data model, we need to introduce the concept of **participation conditions** for entities in relationships.

Mandatory and optional participation

In the university system, we want to keep details of a course even if there are no enrolments for that course, because we expect that there will be enrolments in the future. In other words, we will permit occurrences of Course to exist which are not related to any occurrences of Enrolment. The same is true for Student. We want to keep details of students before they have enrolled for any courses. On the other hand, we would only want to keep details of enrolments provided that the Enrolment occurrence is related to a Student occurrence and a Course occurrence. If this were not the case we could enrol a student for a non-existent course, or enrol a non-existent student! Similarly, if a Student occurrence or Course occurrence is removed from the database, we would want to ensure that all the Enrolment occurrences associated with that Student or Course occurrence are also removed.

We express these semantics by saying that the Enrolled and StudiedBy relationships are **mandatory** with respect to the Enrolment entity. Equivalently, we can say that Enrolment is mandatory with respect to StudiedBy and mandatory with respect to Enrolled. That is to say, each Enrolment occurrence must *always* participate in an occurrence of each of these relationships. The opposite of mandatory is **optional**. An entity is optional with respect to a relationship if each entity occurrence *may* (optionally) participate in an occurrence of the relationship.

Notice that a relationship that is mandatory with respect to one of its related entities may be optional with respect to the other. This is not an inconsistency. For example, Enrolled is mandatory with respect to Enrolment but optional with respect to Student. This means simply that each Enrolment occurrence must be related to a Student occurrence (i.e. each enrolment must be associated with a particular student) but that not every Student occurrence need be related to an Enrolment occurrence (i.e. a student does not have to be enrolled on any courses).

Figure 4.1 shows the notation used for all possible combinations of optional and mandatory participation conditions, in the case of the Counsels relationship. The open circle stands for optional; the black blob stands for mandatory. When neither symbol appears on the relationship line, the relationship is said to be **uncommitted**.

The four cases shown in Figure 4.1 may be interpreted as follows:

(a) Optional participation conditions for both Student and Staff in the Counsels relationship. A member of staff *may* counsel students and a student *may* be counselled by a member of staff. Hence a member of staff may counsel no students, one student or more than one student. A student may have no member of staff as a counsellor. If a student is counselled, he/she must be counselled by just one member of staff.

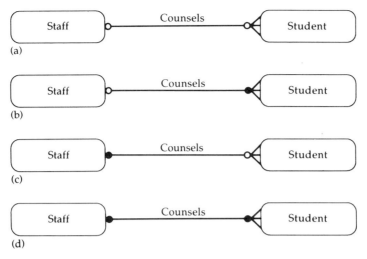

Figure 4.1 The possible mandatory and optional participation conditions for the Counsels relationship.

(b) Optional participation for Staff in the Counsels relationship and mandatory participation for Student in the Counsels relationship. A member of staff *may* counsel students (hence, again, staff may counsel no, one or many students), but a student *must* have just one counsellor.

(c) Mandatory participation for Staff in the Counsels relationship and optional participation for Student in the Counsels relationship. A member of staff *must* counsel at least one student and may counsel many. A student *need not* be counselled by a member of staff and has at most one counsellor.

(d) Mandatory participation for both entities in the Counsels relationship. A member of staff *must* counsel at least one student and may counsel many and a student *must* have just one counsellor.

SAQ 4.2 Given the data requirements of the university system (in Section 2.2), which of the above combinations of optional and mandatory participation conditions do you think is the correct one for the Counsels relationship? Justify your answer with reference to the data requirements.

Solution Case (b) is the one that corresponds to the requirement that 'each staff member may act as a counsellor ... each student has one counsellor'. ∎

SAQ 4.3 Draw an E–R diagram for the following requirement using the entities Patient and Ward and the relationship OccupiedBy:

When in hospital, a patient must occupy a ward. A ward may be occupied by one or more patients or it may be unoccupied.

Solution

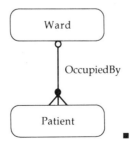

∎

Occurrences can be used to demonstrate that a relationship is optional, but they cannot be used to demonstrate that a relationship is mandatory. Consider the portion of the university database shown in the E–R occurrence diagram of Figure 4.2.

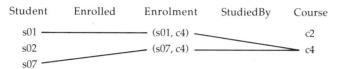

Figure 4.2 E–R occurrence diagram for part of the university database.

Figure 4.2 illustrates the case when the participation conditions relating to Student in the Enrolled relationship and to Course in the StudiedBy relationship are both optional. This may be deduced from the fact that Course occurrence c2 is not related to any occurrences of Enrolment and Student occurrence s02 is not related to any occurrences of Enrolment. We cannot, however, make the statement that Enrolment is mandatory with respect to the Enrolled and StudiedBy relationships on the basis of the occurrences which we have in Figure 4.2.

SAQ 4.4 Why can we not infer from Figure 4.2 alone that StudiedBy and Enrolled are mandatory with respect to Enrolment?

Solution It may just be chance that the given occurrences happen to participate in the Enrolled and StudiedBy relationships. The occurrence diagram does not show the situation if the whole database were represented or what might happen if the database were to change. ∎

SAQ 4.5 Given the data occurrences in Figure 4.2, would (s02, c3) be a valid occurrence of Enrolment if Enrolment is mandatory with respect to the Enrolled and StudiedBy relationships?

Solution No. Course c3 is not a current occurrence of the Course entity so the mandatory participation condition is not satisfied. ∎

Participation conditions are particularly important semantic constraints, because a mandatory participation condition effectively says that no occurrence of this entity will be allowed unless it participates in this relationship. Mandatory participation conditions are, thus, highly restrictive and should be imposed on the EAR conceptual data model only after careful thought. However, they are very effective for maintaining integrity.

Usually, participation conditions are represented on the E–R diagram only towards the end of the data modelling process. The completed EAR model must include participation conditions for all the entities with respect to all their relationships. However, in the early stages of data modelling it is usual to leave out the participation conditions unless they are particularly important. Such detail is not required in the early stages of modelling and would complicate the diagram unnecessarily.

Inclusivity and exclusivity

We now consider semantics associated with the participation of an entity in more than one relationship.

Consider the possible extension to the university system shown in Figure 4.3, which illustrates that, in addition to tutoring enrolments, a member of staff may also examine courses. Further, suppose that the university has a rule which says that if a member of staff tutors any students on a course then the member of staff must also examine that course and vice versa. How can we represent this rule in the EAR model?

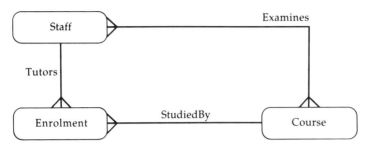

Figure 4.3 Staff involved in an Examines relationship.

If Tutors and Examines were both mandatory for Staff then every Staff occurrence would participate in both relationships. However, with the example in Figure 4.3, this is not the case, since we know from the data requirements for the university system (Section 2.2) that Staff is optional with respect to Tutors. So making both relationships mandatory with respect to staff is not appropriate. What we need to do is to impose a further condition on the EAR model, namely that Tutors and Examines are **inclusive** relationships with respect to Staff – if a Staff occurrence participates in one then it must participate in both relationships. Inclusivity can be extended to any number of relationships.

The opposite of an inclusive relationship is an **exclusive** relationship. This specifies that an entity occurrence may participate in *at most one* of a set of relationships. An example of an exclusive relationship is shown in Figure 4.4. This is another possible extension to the university system which allows for courses which are not yet available for study. A Course occurrence may be InProductionBy a CourseTeam occurrence. In this case a Course occurrence *may* participate either in the StudiedBy relationship *or* in the InProductionBy relationship *or* in neither, but it cannot participate in both relationships. We thus need to impose the condition that these relationships are exclusive with respect to Course. Then participation by a Course occurrence in one of the relationships *precludes* its participation in the other.

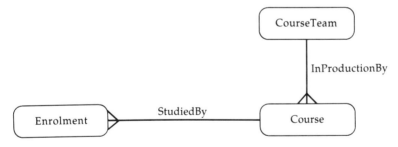

Figure 4.4 Course involved in an InProductionBy relationship.

We show the participation conditions of inclusion and exclusion on the E–R diagram by an arc, to indicate which relationships are being considered, labelled with the word AND to indicate inclusion or the word OR to indicate exclusion. This notation is illustrated in Figure 4.5, for the two examples discussed above.

Exercise 4.2

Write a few sentences to interpret both parts of Figure 4.5, including as much detail as you can deduce from the E–R diagrams. You should assume that the entities and relationships have been defined in the usual way for the university system.

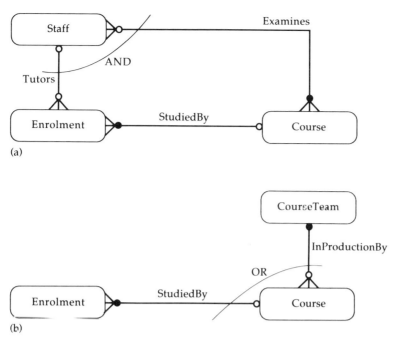

Figure 4.5 Representing (a) inclusive and (b) exclusive relationships.

SAQ 4.6 Is it possible to deduce from Figure 4.5(a) that a member of staff who tutors on a particular course also examines that same course? Explain your answer.

Solution It is not possible to deduce this from Figure 4.5(a). All that we can deduce from the figure is that members of staff who participate in tutoring or examining participate in *both* activities. It would be possible for a member of staff to tutor enrolments on courses different from those that he or she examines. ∎

SAQ 4.6 provides an example of data requirements that cannot be represented on an E–R diagram. This reinforces the point made earlier that, although the E–R diagram is a very significant part of the EAR model, it alone cannot represent all data requirements. Textual descriptions of the entities, attributes and relationships, of the constraints that apply to them and of any assumptions made are also required.

4.3 Dealing with complex relationships

As we intimated in Section 2, any complex relationship (i.e. *m:n* relationship) can be **decomposed** into two relationships, with degree 1:*n* and *m*:1 respectively, with a newly created entity intervening. In other words, an *m:n* relationship can always be replaced by an entity which has a many-to-one relationship with each of the original entities.

You have already seen an example of a decomposition of a complex relationship, the Studies relationship between Student and Course in Figure 2.4. This Studies relationship represented the possibility that any one student could study more than one course and that any one course could be studied by more than one student. We found it useful in that case to decompose the Studies relationship by introducing the entity Enrolment which has the relationship Enrolled with Student and the relationship StudiedBy with Course. Enrolled has degree 1:*n*, representing the fact that one student may enrol for several courses.

Similarly StudiedBy has degree 1:*n* (or 1:*m* if you prefer), representing the fact that a course may be studied by many students.

The identifier of the entity used to decompose a relationship can always be chosen to be the composite of the identifiers of the original pair of entities (though there may be other candidate identifiers). For example, if StudentId is the identifier of Student and CourseCode is the identifier of Course then the identifier of Enrolment may be chosen to be the composite attribute (StudentId, CourseCode).

We can now go a stage further by asserting that when a many-to-many relationship is replaced by an entity and two one-to-many relationships, and provided that the identifier of the new entity is the composite of the identifiers of the original pair of entities, then it is always *mandatory* for the new entity to participate in each of the new relationships. The participation conditions for the original entities with respect to the new relationships remain the same as they were for the old, undecomposed relationship. For example, the old Studies relationship would have been optional with respect to both Student and Course, because a student need not study any courses and a course need not be studied by any students. Hence the new decomposed relationships Enrolled and StudiedBy remain optional with respect to Student and Course respectively, but are both mandatory with respect to Enrolment.

We can now complete the E–R diagram for this portion of the university system as shown in Figure 4.6.

Figure 4.6 The decomposed Studies relationship.

The ability to decompose complex relationships is very useful as it helps us to discover entities and relationships which may otherwise have been overlooked. However, it is perfectly acceptable to have complex relationships in the final E–R diagram of an EAR model. A complex relationship still means the same thing as the entity and the pair of simple relationships which replace it. Providing the entity representing the decomposed relationship has no attributes other than its identifier and is not involved in any relationships with any other entities, leaving it represented as a complex relationship does not cause any problems.

An example of the retention of a many-to-many relationship in an E–R diagram is shown in Figure 4.7. This describes another possible extension to the university system, representing the data requirements that a course may be produced in more than one faculty and that a faculty can produce many courses. There is no data to record about the possible Faculty:Course entity that would be created by decomposing the relationship, nor are there any other relationships which involve such an entity. Thus the many-to-many relationship can be left represented as a complex relationship.

Figure 4.7 Courses produced by more than one faculty.

The advantage of decomposing complex relationships — and one which should not be underestimated — is that it highlights the entities required to represent them and forces the data modeller to consider any possible attributes of such entities, and their relationships with other entities. When developing an EAR model, *all m:n* relationships should be decomposed and examined before a deliberate decision is taken to restore the original (complex) relationship, if that is appropriate.

Exercise 4.3

Suppose we have the following occurrences of data in the university database: s01 is taking c4, s05 is taking c2 and c7, s07 is taking c4.

(a) Draw an E–R occurrence diagram using the *m:n* Studies relationship between Student and Course

(b) Draw an E–R occurrence diagram using the Enrolment entity (which has the identifier (StudentId, CourseCode)) and the relationships Enrolled between Student and Enrolment and StudiedBy between Course and Enrolment.

(c) Write out the occurrences of the Studies relationship and demonstrate that they are equivalent to the occurrences of the Enrolment entity.

(d) Explain why we are able to make the assertion that Enrolled and StudiedBy are mandatory with respect to Enrolment.

We may convince ourselves that we have not lost any relationship information when a relationship is decomposed by considering how we would find out which courses are studied by a particular student using the decomposed model. (In the undecomposed model this information is available directly from the Studies relationship.) Consider, for example, how we would now find the names of all the courses taken by student s05. Using the Enrolled relationship we find the Enrolment occurrences (s05, c2) and (s05, c7), as shown in the solution to Exercise 4.3. Then, using the StudiedBy relationship we find the Course occurrences identified by c2 and c7. Finally, the names of these courses are found as attribute values in the Course occurrences identified by c2 and c7.

SAQ 4.7 How would you find the names of all the students taking the course c4, using the data in Exercise 4.3?

Solution From the given Course occurrence, identified by c4, the Enrolment occurrences (s01, c4) and (s07, c4) are found using the StudiedBy relationship. From these Enrolment occurrences, the Enrolled relationship yields the Student occurrences identified by s01 and s07. An attribute value in each Student occurrence is the student's name. ∎

Exercise 4.4

In the hospital inpatient system, there is an *m:n* relationship, Treats, between the entities Doctor and Patient, as expressed by the portion of the data requirements 'each doctor may treat several patients and a patient may be treated by a number of doctors'. Produce EAR models for this part of the hospital inpatient system in the following two equivalent ways:

(a) representing Treats as a complex relationship;

(b) representing Treats by two simple relationships and an entity called Treatment.

Each model should consist of an E–R diagram, including participation conditions, and entity definitions (see the solutions to Exercises 3.6 and 3.8 for a description of the entities Doctor and Patient and their likely entity definitions).

4.4 Recursive relationships

A **recursive relationship** is one in which an entity has a relationship with itself. That is to say, each relationship occurrence is between two occurrences of the same entity type. Recursive relationships have the same characteristics of degree and participation conditions as non-recursive relationships.

For example, in the data requirements for the hospital inpatient system it was stated that some nurses supervise other nurses. This would be represented in the E–R diagram as shown in Figure 4.8, which shows that one Nurse occurrence may supervise many Nurse occurrences. The participation conditions show that a nurse does not have to be a supervisor or a supervised nurse.

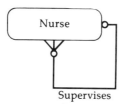

Supervises

Figure 4.8 Recursive relationship for Nurse.

Recursive relationships crop up quite often, particularly with regard to this superordinate/subordinate type of relationship. For example, in a manufacturing environment, one component is manufactured from other components, a department may consist of other subdepartments, and so on.

In the following exercise you will see how a recursive relationship can sometimes be avoided by the use of distinct entity subtypes.

Exercise 4.5 ——————————————————————

In a farm, it is required to record details of the ewes and of the rams with which they have been mated. A ram may be mated with many ewes and a ewe may mate with many rams.

(a) Draw an E–R diagram for these data requirements using the single entity type Sheep and the relationship MatesWith.

(b) Draw an E–R diagram for these data requirements using the entity type sheep, the entity subtypes Ewe and Ram and the relationship MatesWith.

Recursive relationships can be a convenient way of representing some data requirements in an EAR model, but they offer no general advantage over non-recursive relationships. The decision whether to represent some data requirements with a recursive relationship or not depends on how the entities are viewed. If the relationship is genuinely between occurrences of a single entity, then the entity should only be represented once and the relationship will then be recursive. This is the case of nurses above, where there is an assumption that there is no difference in attributes or relationships (other than the Supervises relationship) between the different types of nurse. Indeed, if nurses who supervise are themselves supervised then entity subtypes such as Supervisor and SupervisedNurse would not be possible. The entities Ewes and Rams in Exercise 4.5, however, have different properties and so the use of entity subtypes represents more of the semantics in the data requirements.

There is often a choice between using a recursive relationship and a single entity and using entity subtypes associated with a non-recursive relationship. The choice of how best to represent the data requirements must be based on conformity with good modelling practice: the model should effectively and efficiently represent as completely as possible the data requirements, using a form of representation which highlights the important features and hides the diversionary details.

4.5 Other conceptual data models

Entity–attribute–relationship models are not the only sort of conceptual data models which exist. There are a number of alternative approaches which are favoured by different writers and practitioners. In the EAR conceptual data model, entities have attributes, but relationships do not. *Entity–relationship–attribute (ERA) conceptual data models*, on the other hand, permit both entities and relationships to have attributes.

Other conceptual data models prefer to use only two of the three constructs adopted by the EAR model. *Entity–relationship models* (as opposed to E–R diagrams), sometimes called *object–relationship (OR) models*, use the notion of an *object* which does not have any attributes but is just a classification of values. The two constructs — objects and relationships — are all that is required in order to represent the data requirements.

One very important feature of the EAR model as we have described it so far is that relationships are represented *simply* and *explicitly* by means of the named relationship line. In the **pure entity** version of the EAR model, however, relationships are represented through *shared attributes*. Pure entity versions of the model may still include an E–R diagram, but in pure entity models this diagram is a useful pictorial representation of the data structure rather than an integral part of the conceptual data model.

For example, in the EAR model of the university system, the Enrolment entity has an attribute CourseCode that is shared with Course and an attribute StudentId that is shared with Student. The existence of these shared attributes means that a relationship automatically exists between Enrolment and Course (through the shared CourseCode) and between Enrolment and Student (through the shared StudentId). In fact we used the existence of these shared attributes in order to demonstrate that Enrolment had a mandatory participation condition with respect to StudiedBy and Enrolled (see Exercise 4.3). The shared attributes arose from the technique of decomposing complex relationships. In pure entity versions of the model, *all* relationships are represented by shared attributes and thus relationship lines on a pure entity E–R diagram are simply a convenient notation. They do not represent any of the semantics of the data requirements. In the conventional EAR model, the relationship lines of the E–R diagram are an important semantic construct of the model.[13]

Our choice of the EAR model as the conceptual data model for detailed study is a pragmatic one. It is a simple, yet rich conceptual data model which is widely used in practice in the UK. The EAR model permits entities, but not relationships, to have attributes and represents relationships by means of the named line, rather than through shared attributes. However, this is not to say that entities in the EAR model never have shared attributes. Sometimes it is quite natural to recognize that a property of one entity is also a property of another entity, and, as we have seen, the identifiers of entities created from complex relationships share attributes with the entities in the original relationships.

---

[13] There is an exercise on producing a pure entity model in the next section.

4.6 Summary of section

In this section we have examined the concept of a relationship in the entity–attribute–relationship conceptual data model. Relationships in the EAR model do not have attributes and are characterized by their degree and participation conditions. Any many-to-many relationship can be decomposed into two new relationships, with degree one-to-many, together with a new entity. The new entity has mandatory participation with respect to the new simple relationships created as a result of this decomposition (provided that the identifier of the new entity is the composite of the identifiers of the original pair of entities). Relationships may exist between any two entities, and may be recursive.

Having completed this section you should now be able to:

1 Illustrate and distinguish between relationship occurrences and relationship types, and infer characteristics of the relationship types from the occurrences.

2 Produce an E–R diagram from a statement of data requirements, showing the degree and participation conditions of the relationships.

3 Decompose any complex relationship into two simple relationships.

4 Describe what is meant by a recursive relationship, and illustrate this with examples.

5 Understand what is meant by a pure entity EAR conceptual data model.

5 MODELLING PRACTICE

Recall from Section 2.1 that an EAR model of a system consists of four components:

1 An E–R diagram.

2 Entity definitions.

3 Relationship definitions.

4 Constraints and assumptions.

So far, in Sections 2–4, we have only looked at parts of the EAR model, not the whole. In particular we have looked at parts of the EAR models for the university and hospital inpatient systems. In this section we shall develop complete EAR models for both these systems and for another system that you have not met before — the hockey league system.

5.1 The university

The data requirements for the university system (reproduced from Section 2.2) are as follows:

The university system data requirements

A distance learning university needs to keep details of staff and students, the courses which are available and the performances of students on courses. Students are initially registered and issued with a student identification number. Students do not need to enrol for any courses on initial registration. The region which they are in is recorded along with the year of registration and the student's name. Each member of staff has a staff number and name recorded and also belongs to a region. Each staff member may act as a counsellor to one of more students and/or may tutor one or more students on courses. Each student has one counsellor, and may have a tutor for each course on which he/she is enrolled. Staff members may only tutor and counsel students who are located in the same region as the member of staff.

    Each course which is available for study is given a course code, a title and a credit value. This value is 0.5 for a half-credit course and 1 for a full-credit. Each course may have no, one or many, students enrolled on it. Students may not enrol for more than three credits' worth of courses at any one time. A full-credit course may have up to five TMAs (tutor marked assignments) and a half-credit course up to three TMAs. Each TMA is given a number between 1 and 5. The grade which a student obtains (expressed as a mark out of 100) for a given TMA on a given course is recorded.

You have already seen how most of the parts of an EAR model for these data requirements were developed. Starting from the more obvious entities such as Student, Staff, Course and TMAGrade, Enrolment was added to decompose the relationship between Student and Course. Each of these five entities was defined with a name and a list of its attributes, including its identifier underlined. The relationships Counsels, Tutors, Enrolled, StudiedBy and Awarded were identified, the degree of each was specified and the participation conditions were examined for all but the Awarded relationship.

SAQ 5.1 What are the participation conditions for the Awarded relationship?

Solution Awarded is optional with respect to Enrolment, since students are enrolled on courses before they need to submit any TMAs, and mandatory with respect to TMAGrade. ∎

It only remains to identify any constraints and assumptions, and then to put all the parts together.

Exercise 5.1

(a) Identify any constraints contained in the university system data requirements that are not modelled in the E–R diagram, entity definitions and relationship descriptions for the university system.

(b) What assumptions, if any, were made in drawing up the E–R diagram, entity definitions and relationship descriptions for the university system.

We can now therefore formulate the complete EAR model of the university system, as shown in Figure 5.1.

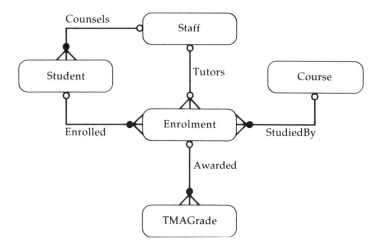

Entity definitions

Student (StudentId, Name, Registered, Region)
Staff (StaffNo, Name, Region)
Course (CourseCode, Title, Credit)
Enrolment (StudentId, CourseCode)
TMAGrade (StudentId, CourseCode, TMANo, Grade)

Relationship descriptions

Name	Comment
Counsels	students being counselled
Tutors	current tutor for enrolment
Enrolled	students taking course
StudiedBy	enrolments for course
Awarded	grades awarded for enrolment

Constraints and assumptions

Staff members may only tutor or counsel students who are located in the same region as the member of staff.

Students may not enrol for more than three credits' worth of courses at any one time.

A full-credit course may have up to five TMAs and a half-credit course up to three TMAs.

Students may not enrol on the same course more than once.

Figure 5.1 Final EAR conceptual data model for the university system.

44

(a) Which relationships in the model in Figure 5.1 are represented by shared attributes and which are not?

(b) In a pure entity version of the EAR model, *all* relationships are represented by shared attributes. Make the necessary changes to the entity definitions in the EAR model in Figure 5.1 in order to turn it into a pure entity model.

5.2 The hospital

We now proceed to develop the full EAR model for the hospital inpatient system by means of a series of exercises, which you should work through carefully in order to gain experience in data modelling. We begin with the data requirements for the system, which are reproduced here from Section 3.4:

The hospital inpatient system data requirements

The hospital is organized into a number of wards, each of which may be empty or may contain one or more patients. Each ward has a ward number and a name recorded, along with the number of beds in that ward. The number of patients occupying a ward cannot exceed the number of beds in the ward. Each ward is staffed by one or more nurses, one of whom is designated to supervise any others on that ward. Nurses have their staff number and name recorded and are assigned to a single ward.

Each patient in the hospital has a patient identification number, and their name, address and date of birth are recorded. Each patient is under the care of a single consultant and is assigned to a single ward. Each consultant is responsible for a number of patients and has a specialism recorded. Details of the junior doctors in the hospital, who are designated either as a registrar or as a houseman, are also recorded. Each doctor in the hospital (whether consultant or junior doctor) has a staff number and name recorded and belongs to a group, known as a team. Each team has a team code, consists of one of more housemen and registrars and is headed by a single consultant. Each consultant heads a team. The number of doctors in each team is recorded.

Each doctor may treat several patients and each patient may be treated by a number of doctors, all of whom must be members of the same team as the consultant who is responsible for the patient. The treatment which a patient receives includes the prescription of a certain dosage of drugs such as paracetamol, morphine, codeine, etc. Each drug has a code. Records are kept of the date and dosage of each drug treatment and of who prescribed it. Only doctors are allowed to prescribe treatment.

Compile a list of likely entities for this system, including any entity subtypes. Suggest an identifier for each entity. Give a one-line clarification of the meaning of the entity, where this is necessary.

Compile a list of likely relationships for this system using the entities in *our* solution to Exercise 5.3, with the exception of the entity Doctor. Use Consultant and JuniorDoctor as ordinary entity types, not as subtypes of Doctor. You may include many-to-many relationships if you find it impossible to decompose them using the given entities. Present your list in tabular form, giving the relationship name, the pair of entities it relates, its degree and a comment amplifying the meaning of the relationship. Do not include the participation conditions.

Exercise 5.5

Draw an E–R diagram for this system, using the entities given in *our* solution to Exercise 5.3, excluding Doctor, and showing the relationships given in our solution to Exercise 5.4. Do not include the participation conditions.

The E–R diagram in the solution to Exercise 5.5 is not entirely to our satisfaction. One area of dissatisfaction concerns the doctors who prescribe treatment. It seems unnecessarily complex to have two relationships. Perhaps we could simplify this part of the diagram by reintroducing Doctor as a supertype for Consultant and JuniorDoctor?

Exercise 5.6

(a) Redraw the part of the E–R diagram that concerns the doctors and the entities with which they have relationships to include the entity type Doctor and the entity subtypes Consultant and JuniorDoctor.

(b) What are the benefits of this representation over the model given in the solution to Exercise 5.5?

(c) Do we still require the IsResponsibleFor relationship?

Exercise 5.7

As a final perspective on this issue, redraw the E–R diagram for the same part of the model as in Exercise 5.6, using the single entity Doctor, with no subtypes. Suggest how the different kinds of doctor can be distinguished from one another on the basis of this redrawn E–R diagram.

Let us now turn our attention to the inclusion of Drug in the model. The data requirements specify that 'treatment … includes the prescription of a certain dosage of drugs … records are kept of the date and dosage of each drug treatment and of who prescribed it'.

Exercise 5.8

Decompose the *m:n* relationship IncludedIn between Treatment and Drug and name the new entity and relationships. Specify the identifiers of Treatment, of Drug and of the new entity.

Exercise 5.9

We would like to make Dosage an attribute of Treatment/Drug, but there is a problem in identifying against which particular occurrence of Treatment/Drug to record particular values of Dosage.

(a) What is the problem in identifying occurrences of Treatment/Drug against which to record values of Dosage?

(b) How could the problem be resolved?

Following the developments in the last two exercises, we should now take stock. Perhaps our model could be simplified in this Treatment/Drug area? Since our original entity, Treatment, has no attributes other than its identifier, we could replace it by the entity Treatment/Drug, so that Doctor and Patient have relationships directly with Treatment/Drug. However, for simplicity of naming entities, let us rename Treatment/Drug to be simply Treatment, noting that Treatment is now defined as:

Treatment (<u>StaffNo, PatientId, DrugCode, Date</u>, Dosage)

Thus Treatment now has the meaning that it is a prescription by a particular doctor for a particular patient of a particular drug on a particular date. (Formerly it meant treatment of a patient by a doctor, regardless of the drug(s) prescribed or the date.) We are making the assumption that a doctor never prescribes the same drug to the same patient more than once on the same date. We will record this as an assumption made during the modelling.

Exercise 5.10

Put together the developments which we have made to the model, namely the identification of the Treatment entity by the identifier (StaffNo, PatientId, DrugCode, Date) and the inclusion of Consultant and JuniorDoctor as entity subtypes of Doctor, and produce a revised E–R diagram for the hospital inpatient system. Include all the participation conditions.

Exercise 5.11

Complete the EAR model for the hospital inpatient system by writing the entity definitions, the relationship descriptions, the constraints and the assumptions in the style of the EAR model for the university system (Figure 5.1).

5.3 The hockey league

In this subsection, you will be required to do the data modelling with only a little guidance from us. The data requirements for the hockey league system are presented below, split into three parts — fixtures, registration and performance. You will be asked to develop an EAR model for each part before bringing them together into a single model of the hockey league system.

The hockey league system data requirements

A hockey league needs to record data in order to help in the control of clubs and players and in the scheduling and recording of results of matches for a season.

Fixtures

Each season, a set of fixtures involving the 26 clubs in the league is drawn up. A fixture is a match involving just two of the clubs in the league, one of which is playing at home (designated as the home club) and the other of which is playing away (designated as the away club). Each club in the league will play two matches against each of the other clubs; in one match it will be the home club and in the other match it will be the away club. Each club may play only one match on any given day. A fixture/results table is produced, a portion of which is shown in Figure 5.2. Clubs are given identification codes, cb01–cb26. Each club also has a name.

Date	HomeClubCode	AwayClubCode	HomeGoals	AwayGoals
1/10/90	cb03	cb17	3	2
1/10/90	cb07	cb09	1	1
1/10/90	cb01	cb20	4	5
1/10/90	cb15	cb08	2	0
8/11/90	cb17	cb03		
8/11/90	cb20	cb01		

Figure 5.2 A portion of the fixture/results table for the hockey league.

Registration

Clubs must be registered with the league, and may do so before they have acquired any players. Each club must register each of its players; each player must be registered with a club. Apart from a player identification code, such as pl124, players names are also recorded. It is possible for players to be transferred between clubs, and the system records details of all such transfers. Each transfer involves one player, the club which the player comes from, the club which the player goes to, and the date of the transfer. For example, player pl124 was transferred from club cb14 to club cb16 on 05/02/90.

Performance

Each time a match is played, data about the players who took part in the match and their performance in the match, such as the number of goals that they scored and the position that they played, are recorded. Each player will typically take part in more than one match but need not take part in any. Any disciplinary offences, such as a player being sent off or cautioned during a match, are also recorded.

Each of the five exercises below should take up to twenty minutes to complete, and you are strongly urged to spend that time before looking at our solution. Even if you seem to be going awry, you should persevere. Remember that producing an E–R diagram helps you to understand the data requirements.

Exercise 5.12 ————————————————

Produce an EAR conceptual data model for the Fixtures part of the hockey league system. Your model should consist of an E–R diagram showing all the entities and relationships, including the degree and participation conditions of each relationship, entity definitions and relationship descriptions. Do not for the moment attempt to specify any constraints or assumptions.

Some comments on the solution to Exercise 5.12 may be helpful.

Club is clearly an entity as it has an identifier, ClubCode, and a name. You may have identified Match as an entity, or you may have identified a recursive *m:n* Plays relationship between Clubs. If you decomposed that relationship, you will have discovered the Match entity.

The attributes of Match are clear from the part of the fixture/results table provided: HomeClubCode, AwayClubCode, Date, HomeGoals and AwayGoals. You should also have recognized that the identifier of Match is (HomeClubCode, AwayClubCode). Date is not required as part of the identifier because the data requirements state that 'each club ... will play two matches against each of the other clubs; in one match it will be the home club and in the other match it will be the away club'. (HomeClubCode, AwayClubCode) will therefore uniquely identify each occurrence of Match.

SAQ 5.2 What constraint is automatically imposed on the system by our choice of Match identifier (and hence need not be recorded separately as a constraint)?

Solution Each club can play every other club at most once at home and at most once away in a season. ■

Exercise 5.13

What constraints and assumptions need to be added to the EAR model of the Fixtures part of the hockey league system developed in the solution to Exercise 5.12.

Exercise 5.14

Produce an EAR conceptual data model for the Registration part of the hockey league system. You model should include any constraints and assumptions.

Again, some comments on the solution to Exercise 5.14 may be helpful.

Club is clearly an entity required in this part too. In addition you should have identified Player as an entity, as it has a clear identifier, PlayerId, and a second attribute of Name. You should also have recognized the entity Transfer as something of interest, and having the attributes FromClubCode, ToClubCode, PlayerId, Date and possibly other attributes. You may have had some difficulty in deciding what the identifier should be. Clearly the club codes are insufficient because several players could be transferred between them in the same season. Similarly the player identification code alone is also inadequate because the player could be transferred more than once. It would seem fairly unlikely that a player could be transferred to or from the same club more than once in a season, so an identifier consisting of, say, (FromClubCode, PlayerId) or (ToClubcode, PlayerId) might be adequate. However, we have chosen the identifier (FromClubCode, ToClubCode, PlayerId) as this will uniquely identify all transfers unless a player returned to the original club and then subsequently repeated the original transfer. This seems highly unlikely. Notice, however, that this produces an assumption that the same player cannot be transferred between the same pair of clubs in the same direction more than once in a season.

You may initially have identified only one relationship between Club and Transfer, but you should have decomposed this relationship into the two 1:n relationships we have called From and To.

The constraint on the codes of clubs involved in a transfer is similar to the constraint on the codes of clubs involved in a match identified in the solution to Exercise 5.13.

Exercise 5.15

Produce an EAR conceptual data model for the Performance part of the hockey league system.

Once more, we comment on the solution to Exercise 5.15.

The entities Match and Player are clearly required here. A player can play in many matches and a match involves many players. There is, thus, a complex relationship between Match and Player, each occurrence of which represents the performance of one player in one match. This complex relationship should be decomposed, to give the new entity Performance and the two new relationships we have named Gives and In. The position played by a player, the number of goals scored by a player and any disciplinary offences committed by a player are attributes of Performance.

The relationship In has optional participation with respect to Match because the fixture details of Match are recorded before performance details are available.

Exercise 5.16

Combining together the solutions to Exercises 5.12, 5.13, 5.14 and 5.15, produce an EAR conceptual data model for the whole of the hockey league system.

5.4 Summary of section

In this section we have concentrated on developing expertise in constructing EAR conceptual data models.

Having completed this section you should now be able to produce a complete EAR model from a statement of the data requirements for a system of a level of complexity similar to the university, hospital inpatient or hockey league systems.

SOLUTIONS TO THE EXERCISES

Solution 1.1

The following models can be identified:

- The sketches are relatively high-level, informal models which are suitable for communicating with colleagues and for exploring alternative designs.

- The scale drawings are formal, precise models which express the meaning of the sketches in a form suitable for communicating with the model-maker.

- The scale models are abstractions, concentrating on shape, which are suitable for marketing personnel to comment on and for testing the designs in a wind tunnel.

Solution 1.2

(a) The designer did not produce scale drawings immediately because it would be unwise to produce such a precise, low-level model as a scale drawing before alternative designs have been explored and general agreement has been obtained at a higher level of abstraction.

(b) The scale drawings were not sent to marketing personnel because they would probably not be familiar with that type of representation. The significant aspect of the car for the purpose of getting the reaction of marketing personnel is shape, so a scale model is a more suitable representation for such personnel.

(c) A scale model is suitable for testing in a wind tunnel because it possesses the significant features of the car in terms of such testing (i.e. shape) while excluding immaterial details (such as the design of the car interior).

Solution 2.1

(a) The five entities that we have identified from the data requirements are: Patient, ClinicAppointment, Consultant, Ward and Nurse, as these are all things which are of interest in the data requirements and about which data is to be kept.

(b) The five relationships that we have identified, and their degrees, are shown in the table below.

Your names for the relationships will probably differ slightly from ours. The order of the entities in each relationship may be the reverse of ours, but if so the degree must also be reversed (i.e. many-to-one rather than one-to-many). The degree of each relationship is found as follows:

- A patient many have many clinic appointments, but each clinic appointment is for just one patient. Hence Patient:ClinicAppointment is one-to-many.

- A consultant has many clinic appointments, but each clinic appointment is for just one consultant. Hence Consultant:Clinic Appointment is one-to-many.

- A ward has many patients in it, but each patient is located in a single ward. Hence Ward:Patient is one-to-many.

- A patient is under the care of a single consultant, but each consultant is responsible for many patients. Hence Consultant:Patient is one-to-many.

- A Nurse is assigned to just one ward, but a ward is staffed by a number of nurses. Hence Ward:Nurse is one-to-many.

(c) The E–R diagram based on the entities and relationships in (a) and (b) is shown below.

Relationship	First entity	Second entity	Degree
Attends	Patient	ClinicAppointment	one-to-many
Takes	Consultant	ClinicAppointment	one-to-many
OccupiedBy	Ward	Patient	one-to-many
IsResponsibleFor	Consultant	Patient	one-to-many
StaffedBy	Ward	Nurse	one-to-many

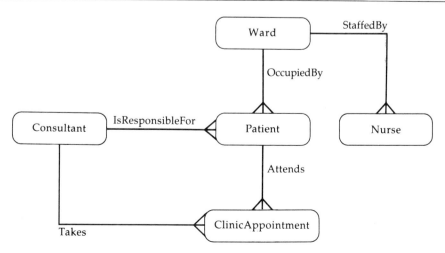

Your E–R diagram will depend on the entities and relationships you identified in (a) and (b), but it should be similar to the one given.

Solution 2.2

(a) The entity occurrences (in order of appearance) are: Akeroyd, Semantics, Ellis, Syntax, Pragmatics and Reeves.

(b) The two entity types are Student and Course. There are three occurrences of each.

(c) The relationship type is Studies. There are six occurrences of this relationship type.

(d)

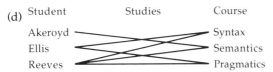

(e) Studies is a many-to-many relationship, because we have at least one example of a student who studies more than one course (Ellis studies Syntax and Pragmatics) and at least one example of a course which is studied by more than one student (Syntax is studied by Ellis and Reeves).

Solution 3.1

(a) Clinic is an entity. Its attributes are Date, ClinicName and DayName.

   Consultant is also an entity. It has attributes ConsultantName, Title and Specialism.

(b) Clinic cannot be identified solely by ClinicName as the data requirements tell us that each clinic happens several times a week. Therefore we must consider using a composite identifier. One possibility is (ClinicName, DayName); however, this is not suitable if we want to keep data about clinics over more than one week. Another possibility is (ClinicName, Date), which is suitable as it uniquely distinguishes between clinic occurrences — i.e. the dates when the clinic is run. This identifier is unique because the same clinic never runs more than once on the same date. However, if the system were to evolve so that there was more than one clinic of the same type on the same day then we would have to find another identifier.

   Consultant can be identified by ConsultantName, since we know the names are distinct at present. However, this means that the system could not evolve to accommodate more than one consultant with the same name, without changing the identifier. Any composite identifier based on the three attributes of Consultant would suffer from the same deficiency.

(c) Ear, Nose and Throat and Antenatal are values of the attribute ClinicName, but they do not identify occurrences of the Clinic entity since they do not include the date. Watson, Owen and Cunningham are values of the attribute ConsultantName and identify occurrences of Consultant (at present). The attribute Title has values Dr and Mr and these values do not identify occurrences.

Solution 3.2

Enrolment is an entity representing students' enrolments on courses. So far, we have not identified any attributes for Enrolment. However, since each Enrolment occurrence relates to one student and one course, two suitable attributes are StudentId and CourseCode. Since StudentId uniquely identifies a Student occurrence and CourseCode uniquely identifies a Course occurrence, a suitable identifier for Enrolment is the composite (StudentId, CourseCode). These two attributes are the minimum required to distinguish between occurrences of the Enrolment entity.

   (StudentId, CourseCode) will only be unique, however, as long as the system includes current enrolments only or as long as students are not permitted to enrol on the same course more than once; for, if enrolments over a number of years were recorded and if a student could enrol on the same course more than once, then the value of (StudentId, CourseCode) would not be sufficient to distinguish between these Enrolment occurrences.

Solution 3.3

EnrolmentNumber is clearly a possible identifier for Enrolment in either case since the data requirements state that 'each enrolment [occurrence] is given a unique [value of] enrolment number'.

(a) If data on current enrolments only is kept then we know (from the solution to Exercise 3.2) that (StudentId, CourseCode) is also a possible identifier for Enrolment. In this situation either identifier would be acceptable, although EnrolmentNumber is the more obvious choice. Hence both (StudentId, CourseCode) and EnrolmentNumber are *candidate identifiers* for Enrolment.

(b) If data on previous enrolments is also to be kept then (StudentId, CourseCode) is no longer a candidate identifier unless there is a prohibition on students studying the same course more than once (see the solution to Exercise 3.2). Since no such prohibition is specified, EnrolmentNumber is the only possible identifier for Enrolment.

Solution 3.4

The identifier of TMAGrade is (StudentId, CourseCode, TMANo).

Clearly TMANo on its own cannot be the identifier since it only has a value set of {1, 2, 3, 4, 5} and hence only five occurrences can be distinguished throughout the whole database. Furthermore, Grade cannot be used as (part of) an identifier since it need not have a value at any given time, contradicting the existence criterion for identifiers. However, we know that there can be up to five TMA occurrences for *each student on each course* (i.e. for each Enrolment). Since (StudentId, CourseCode) identifies Enrolment and there are at most five TMAs for each Enrolment, (StudentId, CourseCode, TMANo) is a minimum combination of attributes the values of which distinguish between occurrences of TMAGrade. Hence this composite must be the identifier for TMAGrade.

(If you are unconvinced by this solution, write out some occurrences of TMAGrade and convince yourself that each occurrence has a different value for (StudentId, CourseCode, TMANo).)

Solution 3.5

Staff (StaffNo, Name, Region)
Enrolment (StudentId, CourseCode)
TMAGrade (StudentId, CourseCode, TMANo, Grade)

Solution 3.6

Our list of entities is given below:

Ward	a ward in the hospital
Patient	a patient *currently* staying in the hospital
Nurse	a nurse in the hospital
Doctor	a doctor in the hospital (who may be a consultant or a junior doctor)
Team	a group of doctors who work together
Consultant	a doctor who is a consultant
JuniorDoctor	a doctor who is not a consultant
Drug	a drug that may be prescribed by a doctor

Your list should not be significantly different from this. Other entities that you may have identified include Treatment, Registrar and Houseman. Treatment is a perfectly reasonable choice, as we shall see later — but for the moment we omit it from our list. The data requirements do not make it clear whether Registrar and Houseman need to be separate entities or whether they are values of an attribute, Position say, of JuniorDoctor. We shall choose the latter. It is possible that you did not consider Consultant and JuniorDoctor be separate entities, but took them to be values of an attribute of Doctor; this again would have been a reasonable assumption, but not one that we shall pursue for reasons which will become clear later.

Solution 3.7

Entity	Identifier
Ward	WardNo
Patient	PatientId
Nurse	StaffNo
Doctor	StaffNo
Team	TeamCode
Consultant	StaffNo
JuniorDoctor	StaffNo
Drug	DrugCode

Solution 3.8

(a) The degrees are as follows:

(i) Treats between Doctor and Patient is a many-to-many relationship.

(ii) HeadedBy between Team and Consultant is a one-to-one relationship.

(iii) ConsistsOf between Team and JuniorDoctor is a one-to-many relationship.

(b)

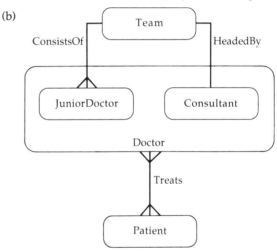

Team (TeamCode, NumberOfDoctors)
Patient (PatientId, Name, Address, DateOfBirth)
Doctor (StaffNo, Name, ...)
Consultant (StaffNo, Specialism, ...)
JuniorDoctor (StaffNo, Position, ...)

Your list of attributes for each entity may include other possible attributes but should include at least those listed.

Solution 4.1

(a)

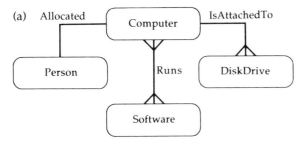

(b) Allocated is one-to-one since nobody is allocated more than one computer and no more than one person is allocated to any computer.

IsAttachedTo is one-to-many since a computer may have one or more disk drives, but each disk drive is attached to only one computer at a time.

Runs is many-to-many since a computer runs many pieces of software and a piece of software may be run on more than one computer.

Solution 4.2

(a) Staff may tutor one or more enrolments and may examine one or more courses. A course must be examined by one member of staff and may be examined by many members of staff. A course may be studied by no, one or many enrolments. An enrolment must be related to one course and may be related to one member of staff. A member of staff does not have to participate in either tutoring or examining, but if they do one they must do both.

(b) A course may be studied by no, one or many enrolments or may be in production by a single course team. A course team may produce many courses, but must be associated with at least one course. An enrolment must be related to exactly one course. A course may be *either* in production *or* available to be studied *or* neither, but it cannot be in production and available to be studied.

Solution 4.3

(a)

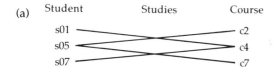

(b)

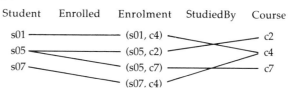

(c) The four occurrences of Studies are represented by the pairs (s01, c4), (s05, c2), (s05, c7), and (s07, c4), which are identical to the four occurrences of Enrolment.

(d) Since each value of the identifier of Enrolment includes a value of both StudentId and CourseCode, there must be a relationship occurrence for each occurrence of Enrolment with both an occurrence of Student (based on the value of StudentId) and an occurrence of Course (based on the value of CourseCode). Since each occurrence of Enrolment must be related to an occurrence of Student and to an occurrence of Course, the entity type Enrolment must always be related to the entity type Student and to the entity type Course. Enrolment is thus mandatory with respect to Enrolled (the relationship between Enrolment and Student) and with respect to StudiedBy (the relationship between Enrolment and Course).

Solution 4.4

(a)

Doctor ├──>○── Treats ──○<──┤ Patient

Doctor (StaffNo, Name, ...)
Patient (PatientId, Name, Address, DateOfBirth)

(b)

Doctor   Patient

Prescribes   Treatment   Receives

Doctor (StaffNo, Name, ...)
Patient (PatientId, Name, Address, DateOfBirth)
Treatment (StaffNo, PatientId, ...)

Your solutions should be similar to ours except that you may have given the relationships in (b) different names and that you may have included more attributes in the entity definitions of Doctor and Treatment.

Solution 4.5

(a)

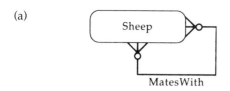

(b)

MatesWith

Ewe — Ram

Sheep

Solution 5.1

(a) There are three constraints that have not been otherwise modelled:

• Staff members may only tutor or counsel students who are located in the same region as the member of staff.

• Students may not enrol for more than three credits' worth of courses at any one time.

• A full-credit course may have up to five TMAs and a half-credit course up to three TMAs.

You may also have considered the value sets for the attributes of the various entities to be constraints on the system that have not otherwise been modelled. Note, however, that value sets for attributes are not considered to be part of the EAR model; they are covered in the next stage of the data modelling process — the production of the logical schema — as you will discover in Part II.2.

(b) One assumption has been made, when deciding on the identifier of Enrolment (see Exercise 3.2):

• Students may not enrol on the same course more than once.

Solution 5.2

(a) Enrolled is represented by StudentId being shared between Student and Enrolment. StudiedBy is represented by CourseCode being shared between Course and Enrolment. Awarded is represented by (StudentId, CourseCode) being shared between Enrolment and TMAGrade. The other two relationships, Counsels and Tutors, are not represented by shared attributes.

(b) The entity definitions which require changing in order to produce a pure entity model of the university system are those which are currently involved in relationships which are not represented by shared attributes, namely Student's relationship with Staff (Counsels) and Staff's relationship with Enrolment (Tutors). The Counsels relationship can be represented by including the identifier of Staff as an attribute of Student. The Tutors relationship can be represented by including the identifier of Staff as an attribute of Enrolment. This gives the following entity definitions for the pure entity model of the university system, where we use CounsellorNo and TutorNo, rather than StaffNo, as the names of the new attributes of Student and Enrolment:

Student (StudentId, Name, Registered, Region, CounsellorNo)
Staff (StaffNo, Name, Region)
Course (CourseCode, Title, Credit)
Enrolment (StudentId, CourseCode, TutorNo)
TMAGrade (StudentId, CourseCode, TMANo, Grade)

Solution 5.3

As with all the solutions to the exercises on the hospital inpatient system in this subsection, you are unlikely to have produced exactly the same solution as we have, particularly with regard to the names you have used for the various entities, etc. However, you should have produced something similar to our solution.

Entity	Identifier	Meaning
Ward	WardNo	ward in hospital
Patient	PatientId	current inpatient
Nurse	StaffNo	nurse on staff list
Doctor	StaffNo	doctor on staff list
Consultant	StaffNo	doctor who is a consultant
JuniorDoctor	StaffNo	doctor who is not a consultant
Team	TeamCode	group of doctors working together
Drug	DrugCode	prescribable drug
Treatment	(StaffNo, PatientId)	treatment of patient by doctor

Solution 5.4

Relationship	Entity pair	Degree	Comment
OccupiedBy	Ward:Patient	1:n	current ward of patient
StaffedBy	Ward:Nurse	1:n	current assignments
Supervises	Nurse:Nurse	1:n	recursive relationship
IsResponsibleFor	Consultant:Patient	1:n	consultants are responsible for patients
ConsistsOf	Team:JuniorDoctor	1:n	excludes consultants
HeadedBy	Team:Consultant	1:1	each consultant heads a team
Prescribes	JuniorDoctor:Treatment	1:n	all junior doctors can prescribe
AlsoPrescribes	Consultant:Treatment	1:n	consultants can also prescribe
Receives	Patient:Treatment	1:n	patients receive treatment
IncludedIn	Drug:Treatment	m:n	drug prescribed in treatment

Notice that separate names are required for Prescribes and AlsoPrescribes because they are relationships between different entities.

The IncludedIn relationship is m:n and cannot be decomposed without introducing another entity.

Solution 5.5

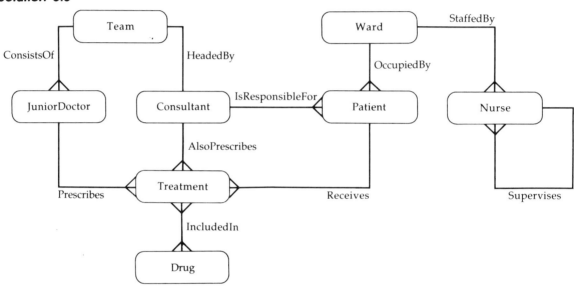

Your diagram should differ from ours only in layout. You should have avoided relationship lines that cross each other.

Check that you have represented all 1:n relationships the right way round.

Solution 5.6

(a)

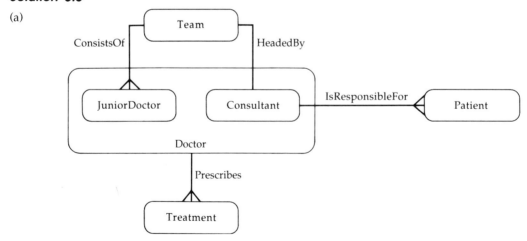

(b) The main benefit is that the Prescribes relationship can now be more simply represented. Furthermore, the mandatory participation condition for treatment with respect to Prescribes can now be imposed on the diagram. *This was not possible* with the representation of Solution 5.5, since Treatment could not be mandatory with respect to Prescribes *and* AlsoPrescribes, but only with one *or* the other. There is also a sense of style involved: the subtype notation is a neater solution.

(c) The IsResponsibleFor relationship *is* still required because it is a relationship between Consultant and Patient and not between Doctor and Patient.

Solution 5.7

The E–R diagram is shown below.

The different kinds of Doctor occurrences can be distinguished by acknowledging the existence of the attribute Position for the entity Doctor. A Position with the value of Consultant is then necessary for a Doctor occurrence to head a team or to participate in the IsResponsibleFor relationship. The other values of Position would be Registrar and Houseman. (You may recall that we recommended the Position attribute for JuniorDoctors in the solution to Exercise 3.6.)

Solution 5.8

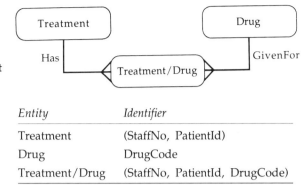

Entity	Identifier
Treatment	(StaffNo, PatientId)
Drug	DrugCode
Treatment/Drug	(StaffNo, PatientId, DrugCode)

Solution 5.9

(a) The entity Treatment/Drug has identifier (StaffNo, PatientId, DrugCode) and cannot have Dosage as an attribute if it is possible for the same doctor to prescribe the same drug to the same patient *on different occasions*. Since it *is* possible that a doctor will prescribe the same drug to the same patient on different occasions, we need to refine our definition of Treatment/Drug.

(b) One solution is to introduce an attribute Date to the identifier of Treatment/Drug. This is a satisfactory solution if the same doctor cannot prescribe the same drug to the same patient on the same date more than once. (If the same doctor is allowed to prescribe the same drug to the same patient more than once on the same date, then we would need to add another attribute, Time say, to the identifier of Treatment/Drug. We shall assume that the addition of Date is sufficient.)

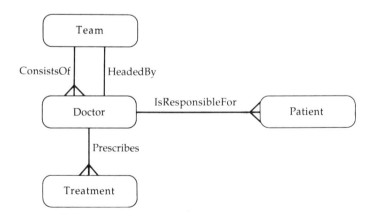

Solution 5.10

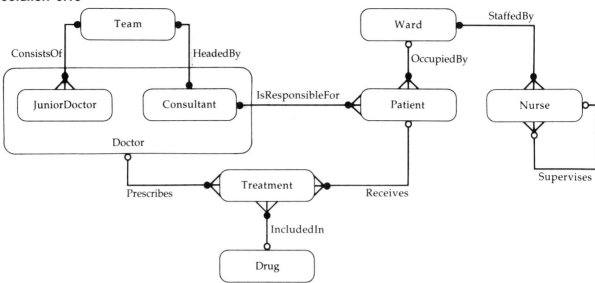

Solution 5.11

Entity definitions

Ward (<u>WardNo</u>, WardName, NumberOfBeds)
Patient (<u>PatientId</u>, PatientName, Address, DateOfBirth)
Nurse (<u>StaffNo</u>, NurseName)
Doctor (<u>StaffNo</u>, DoctorName)
Consultant (<u>StaffNo</u>, Specialism)
JuniorDoctor (<u>StaffNo</u>, Position)
Team (<u>TeamCode</u>, NoOfDoctors)
Drug (<u>DrugCode</u>, DrugName)
Treatment (<u>StaffNo, PatientId, DrugCode, Date</u>, Dosage)

Relationship descriptions

Name	Comment
OccupiedBy	current ward of patient
StaffedBy	current assignments
Supervises	recursive relationship
IsResponsibleFor	consultants are responsible for patients
ConsistsOf	excludes consultants
HeadedBy	each consultant heads a team
Prescribes	all doctors can prescribe
Receives	patients receive treatment
IncludedIn	drug prescribed in treatment

Constraints and assumptions

The number of patients occupying a ward cannot exceed the number of beds in that ward.

The doctor prescribing treatment must be from the same team as the consultant who is responsible for the patient.

The same doctor cannot give the same drug to the same patient more than once on the same day.

Solution 5.12

As with all the solutions to the exercises on the hockey league system in this subsection, you are unlikely to have produced exactly the same solution as we have, particularly with regard to the names you have used for the various entities, etc. However, you should have produced something similar to our solution.

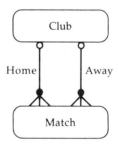

Entity definitions

Club (<u>ClubCode</u>, ClubName)
Match (<u>HomeClubCode, AwayClubCode</u>, Date, HomeGoals, AwayGoals)

Relationship descriptions

Name	Comment
Home	club playing at home
Away	club playing away

Solution 5.13

Constraints and assumptions

Each club may only play one match on any one day.

Each club must play each other club *exactly* once at home and *exactly* once away in a season.

The two clubs involved in a match must be different.

Solution 5.14

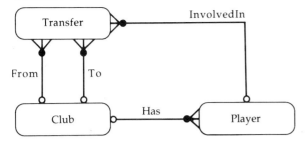

Entity definitions

Club (ClubCode, ClubName)
Player (PlayerId, Name)
Transfer (FromClubCode, ToClubCode, PlayerId, Date)

Relationship descriptions

Name	Comment
Has	player must have a club
From	transfer from club
To	transfer to club
InvolvedIn	player involved in transfer

Constraints and assumptions

The two clubs involved in a transfer must be different.

A player may not be involved in exactly the same transfer more than once in the same season.

Solution 5.15

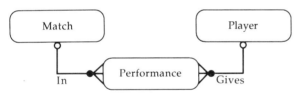

Entity definitions

Player (PlayerId, Name)
Match (HomeClubCode, AwayClubCode, Date, HomeGoals, AwayGoals)
Performance (HomeClubCode, AwayClubCode, PlayerId, GoalsScored, DisciplinaryOffence, PositionPlayed)

Relationship descriptions

Name	Comment
In	Performance:Match relationship
Gives	Player:Performance relationship

Constraints and assumptions

Each player who performs in a match must be registered with either the away club or the home club involved in the match.

The total number of goals recorded as being scored by players during a match must equal the total number of home goals and away goals recorded for the match.

Solution 5.16

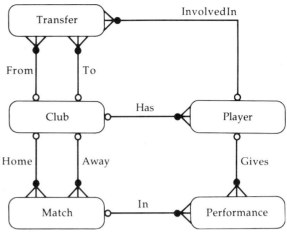

Entity definitions

Club (ClubCode, ClubName)
Match (HomeClubCode, AwayClubCode, Date, HomeGoals, AwayGoals)
Player (PlayerId, Name)
Transfer (FromClubCode, ToClubCode, PlayerId, Date)
Performance (HomeClubCode, AwayClubCode, PlayerId, GoalsScored, DisciplinaryOffence, PositionPlayed)

Relationship descriptions

Name	Comment
Home	club playing at home
Away	club playing away
Has	player must have a club
From	transfer from club
To	transfer to club
InvolvedIn	player involved in transfer
In	Performance:Match relationship
Gives	Player:Performance relationship

Constraints and assumptions

Each club may only play one match on any one day.

Each club must play each other club *exactly* once at home and *exactly* once away in a season.

The two clubs involved in a match must be different.

The two clubs involved in a transfer must be different.

Each player who performs in a match must be registered with either the away club or the home club involved in the match.

The total number of goals recorded as being scored by players during a match must equal the total number of home goals and away goals recorded for the match.

A player may not be involved in exactly the same transfer more than once in the same season.